26 Steps to Heaven

Dedication

'I dedicate this book to Duncan and Sue Collins — two angels on the journey of life.'

26 Steps
to Heaven

An A to Z of
Enlightened Thinking

J. John

H
HODDER

First published in Great Britain in 2007 by Hodder & Stoughton
An Hachette Livre UK company

First published in paperback in 2008

2

A CIP catalogue record for this title is available from the British Library

ISBN 978 0340 95437 9

Typeset in Gill Sans by Avon DataSet Ltd, Bidford on Avon, Warwickshire

Printed and bound in Great Britain by
Clays Ltd, St Ives plc

Hodder & Stoughton policy is to use papers that are natural, renewable and
recyclable products and made from wood grown in sustainable forests. The logging
and manufacturing processes are expected to conform to the environmental
regulations of the country of origin.

Hodder & Stoughton Ltd
338 Euston Road
London NW1 3BH

www.hodderfaith.com

Contents

L leadership · learning · life · loneliness · love · loyalty

M manners · marriage · meanness · mistakes · money · morals

N nature · New Year

O obstacles · opportunity · optimism and pessimism

P passion · patience · peace · perseverance · potential · power · prayer · pride · problems

Q quality · quietness

R resilience · responsibility

S self-control · sincerity · stress · success · suffering

T temptation · thanksgiving · time · truth

U understanding · unselfishness

V values · vision

W wisdom · work · worry

X Xmas

Y youth

Z zeal

Foreword

I hope you enjoy reading this book and I hope the insights will illuminate your thinking. Many of the quotes I have selected reflect the general wisdom of the human race, learned over the ages through the painful process of trial and error. I am very glad to pass them on to you because, as Publius Syrus wrote in 42 BC, 'From the errors of others, a wise man corrects his own.' How wise.

Introduction

Heaven

Do you think much about heaven? Have you been lulled into boredom by the insipid idea that we will be sitting on clouds playing harps?

Are we like the little girl who said, 'Heaven is a nice place, but nobody is in a rush to get there'?

Heaven is one of the most misused religious ideas around today. That is, if you do believe in heaven. Some people take their lead from John Lennon, 'Imagine there's no heaven, it isn't hard to do . . .'

Whatever you believe or don't believe about heaven, I invite you to suspend judgement and wonder with me what the implications might be if what the Bible says is true. Of course, it is true that the idea of heaven has been used as a threat, as some strange distant place, which, if you want to go there someday, 'Well, you just better get your act together so you might be able to bargain yourself in.'

Heaven in the Bible is not a place in the blue beyond. Heaven is God's space; it's the full reality of God. We catch glimpses of God's space all over the world, but it is not established here.

It is not that earth is real and heaven is less real, but rather that what we are living in now is less real compared to what will be. The writer C. S. Lewis talked about this earthly life as being the 'shadowlands'. This life, the colours we see, the good we experience, the joy we have, the pleasures we know – these are as minor shadows compared to the extraordinary colour, beauty, joy and delight of heaven. We haven't seen anything yet – this is just like the warm-up kick-around before the football match really begins.

Earth is really heaven's dress rehearsal.

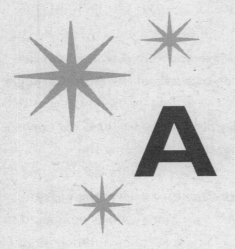

Ability

For better or worse, you must play your own little instrument in the orchestra of life. *Dale Carnegie*

You are the only person on earth who can use your ability. *Zig Ziglar*

They are able because they think they are able. *Virgil*

Genius is the ability to put into effect what is on your mind. *F. Scott Fitzgerald*

Do not let what you cannot do interfere with what you can do. The inventor Thomas Edison was almost deaf, but that didn't hinder him. He focussed on his ability to think creatively (and create). 'If we did all the things we are capable of doing,' reflected Edison, 'we would literally astound ourselves.' We all have ability but what makes the difference is how we use it.

When 20th Century Fox advertised a vacancy in its sales team, one applicant replied: 'I am at present selling furniture at the address below. You may judge my ability as a salesman if you will stop in to see me at anytime, pretending you are interested in buying furniture. When you come in, you can identify me by my black hair. And I will have no way of identifying you. Such salesmanship as I exhibit during your visit, therefore, will be no more than my usual workday approach and not a special effort to impress a prospective employer.' He got the job out of 1500 applicants. That man obviously had ability seasoned with creativity.

Achievement

To leave footprints on the sands of time, wear work shoes. *Anon*

Some of the world's greatest feats were accomplished by people not smart enough to know they were impossible. *Doug Larson*

Farmers who wait for perfect weather never plant. If they watch every cloud, they never harvest.
The Bible, New Living Translation – Ecclesiastes 11:4

Achievement

After all is said and done, there's a lot more said than done. Do not mistake activity for achievement. Most of us can do more than we think we can, but we usually do less than we think we do.

There are four steps to achievement:

- Prepare prayerfully,
- Plan purposefully,
- Proceed positively,
- Pursue persistently.

Failure is the path of least persistence.

Action

There are risks and costs to a programme of action. But these are far less than the long-range risks and costs of comfortable inaction. *John F. Kennedy*

Some people wait so long for their ship to come in, their pier collapses. *John Goddard*

Everyone who got where he is, had to begin where he was. *Robert Louis Stevenson*

Well done is better than well said.
Benjamin Franklin

Action

The following story captures the importance of action. There once were four people named Everybody, Somebody, Anybody and Nobody. An important job had to be done and Everybody was sure that Somebody would do it. Anybody could have done it, but Nobody did it. Somebody got angry with that, because it was Everybody's job. Everybody thought Anybody could do it and that Somebody would do it. But Nobody realised that Everybody thought that Somebody would do it. It ended up that Everybody blamed Somebody when Nobody did what Anybody could have done.

Adversity

Have courage for the great sorrows of life and
patience for the small ones. And when you have
finished your daily task, go to sleep in peace. God is
awake. *Victor Hugo*

Good timber does not grow with ease; the stronger
the wind, the stronger the trees.
J. Willard Marriot

Adversity

A smooth sea never made a skilful mariner. We cannot control all the things that are going to happen. We cannot control the direction of the wind but we can set our sail.

One day, a farmer's donkey fell down into a well. The animal cried piteously for hours as the farmer tried to figure out what to do. Finally, he decided that the animal was old and the well needed to be covered up anyway and that it just wasn't worth it to retrieve the donkey, so he invited all his neighbours to come over and help him. They all grabbed a spade and began to shovel dirt into the well. At first, the donkey realised what was happening and cried horribly. Then, to everyone's amazement, he quietened down. A few shovel loads later, the farmer finally looked down the well and was astonished at what he saw. With every shovel of dirt that hit his back, the donkey was doing something amazing. He would shake it off and take a step up. As the farmer's neighbours continued to shovel dirt on top of the animal, he would shake it off and take a step up. Pretty soon everyone was amazed as the donkey stepped up over the edge of the well and trotted off!

The best way out of a problem is often through it. We must be willing to shake ourselves off and continue upward.

Age

Middle age is actually the prime of life. It just takes a little longer to get primed. Just remember, when you are over the hill, you begin to pick up speed.
Franklin, from 'Peanuts Comic Strip', May 3, 1974

Age is a question of mind over matter. If you don't mind, it doesn't matter. *Satchel Paige*

The first forty years of life give you the text; the next thirty supply the commentary on it.
Arthur Schopenhauer

The Encarta Encyclopaedia defines ageing as the 'irreversible biological change that occurs in all living things with the passing of time, eventually resulting in death'.

The passage of time, what does it mean? The ancient Greeks had two slogans posted over the temple at Delphi. One was 'Know thyself', and the other 'Know thy moment'. Decisive moments in time are denoted by the Greek word *Kairos*. *Kairos* is contrasted with *Chronos* (measured time). *Chronos* is a period, a quantity. *Kairos* is the meaning of that period. *Chronos* is a date – December 25th. *Kairos* is a season – winter. *Chronos* is time to be managed and used. *Kairos* is time to be understood and responded to.

In 1895, the Chancellor of the Exchequer of Great Britain had lunch with a young politician. He told him, 'The experiences of a long life have convinced me that nothing ever happens' (*Chronos*). The young man's name was Winston Churchill. His lifetime of 90 years demonstrated the opposite: that practically everything happens (*Kairos*).

Anger

People who fly into a rage always make a bad landing. *Anon*

The discretion of a man makes him slow to anger, and his glory is to overlook a transgression.
The Bible, New King James Version – Proverbs 19:11

Do not let the sun go down while you are still angry. *The Bible – Ephesians 4:26*

Anger makes our mouths work faster than our minds. That is why the greatest remedy for anger is delay. Remember, our temper is something we never get rid of by losing.

The key to understanding anger is to realise that anger is like fire. Both can be sources of great energy when used rightly but both are lethal if allowed to get out of control.

If, when faced with some problem, we let our anger freely blaze away, then the results will almost certainly be negative. If, on the contrary, we control our anger and focus it on the problem and not the person involved, then good may result. But it is always worth remembering that anger is only one letter away from danger.

Anxiety

Anxiety does not empty tomorrow of its sorrows; it only empties today of its strength.
Corrie Ten Boom

Of all base passions, fear is most accursed.
William Shakespeare

Even tomorrow has two handles. We can take hold of it with the handle of anxiety or the handle of faith. *Henry Ward Beecher*

Anxiety is the space between the 'now' and the 'then'. Never let yesterday use up too much of today. Remember today is the tomorrow you worried about yesterday. A lot of anxiety is often caused by people trying to make decisions before they have sufficient knowledge and information on which to make a decision. Some degree of concern for the future is vital: tomorrow will not look after itself. Yet it is easy to cross the boundary from legitimate concern to anxiety. To be in a state of anxiety is like revving an engine without the clutch being engaged; you get a lot of noise and a great deal of wear and tear but make no progress. It is important to look at the things that face us and divide them into those that we can deal with and those we can't. To be anxious about those things over which we have no control is to wear our lives away with senseless and unprofitable concern.

Arguments

When people agree with me, I always feel that I must be wrong. *Oscar Wilde*

When people are least sure, they are often most dogmatic. *John Galbraith*

People are generally persuaded by the reasons which they have themselves discovered rather than by those which have come to the minds of others. *Blaise Pascal*

Quarrels would not last long if the fault were on one side only. *François de La Rochefoucauld*

There are two equal and opposite dangers with argument. The first danger is that we love arguing so much that even the most trivial matter will provide us with an excuse for an argument. The second danger is that we loathe arguing so much that not even the most serious matter will persuade us into defending our position. Both are wrong; arguments for the sake of arguing are wrong but to fail to argue for what we know is right is just as bad. Truth and love are two good guidelines to the conduct of an argument. We should stop arguing when we cease to be truthful; to have to resort to lies is an admission that we have lost the argument. We should also stop arguing when we have ceased to care for the other person. Arguments fuelled by contempt or hatred are likely to do damage to all involved. It is far better to lose an argument than a friend. If we must argue – and sometimes we must – then we need to make sure that our argument generates far more light than heat.

Attitude

There is very little difference in people. But that little difference makes a big difference. The little difference is attitude. The big difference is whether it is positive or negative. *W. Clement Stone*

It's not so much what happens to us, as what happens in us that counts, or what we think has happened to us. *Tim Hansel*

Always imitate the behaviour of the winners when you lose. *George Meredith*

Everything can be taken away from a person but one thing, the last of the human freedoms – to choose one's attitude in any given circumstance. *Viktor E. Frankl*

An optimist thinks that the glass is half full; a pessimist thinks the glass is half empty. A realist knows that eventually someone is going to have to wash the glass.

There is no denying that we can alter our perspective on life simply by altering our attitudes.

Yes, of course incidents in life can colour our view of life, but we have been given the choice of what the colour of life will be. Life can at times feel like a grindstone, but whether it grinds us down or polishes us up depends on us.

The Greek poet Hermessianes (400 BC) left us a four-word phrase still meaningful today. He wrote, 'As within, so without.' The attitude we have within influences everything else.

Things turn out for the best for people who make the best out of the way things turn out.

B

Beauty

The pursuit of truth and beauty is a sphere of activity in which we are permitted to remain children all our lives. *Albert Einstein*

Beauty is God's handwriting. Welcome it in every face, every day. *Charles Kingsley*

The most beautiful things in the world are the most useless; peacocks and lilies for instance.
John Ruskin

A thing of beauty is a joy forever. *John Keats*

To have beauty is to have only that, but to have goodness is to be beautiful too. *Soppho*

The best and most beautiful things in the world cannot be seen or even touched. They must be felt with the heart. *Helen Keller*

Beauty

To see beauty in something – whether a flower, bird, landscape or person – is to experience something remarkable. Why we feel a sense of beauty remains a mystery. Beauty has no obvious purpose other than to make us feel good and it makes no sense in any view of the world that sees us as no more than molecules, chemicals and genes. Beauty reminds us that there are things in life that we cannot explain. A better way of understanding beauty is to think of the world as being, in some way, like a mirror that reflects the God who made it. Beauty is a reflected glimpse of God.

Belief

Believe in something larger than yourself.
Barbara Bush

Conversion for me was not a Damascus Road Experience. I slowly moved into an intellectual acceptance of what my intuition had always known.
Madeleine L'Engle

All I have seen teaches me to trust the creator for all I have not seen. *Ralph Waldo Emerson*

I would not say I believe. I know. I have had the experience of being gripped by something that is stronger than myself, something that people call God. *Carl Jung*

People readily believe what they want to believe.
Julius Caesar

It is often considered that belief is something that is confined to religious people. The reality is that everybody has beliefs. Some of these are based on good evidence, some of these are little more than hunches, and some of these are mostly wishful thinking. Our beliefs shape who we are and how we react; taken together they make us what we are. Like steel girders in a building, they lie buried below the surface of our lives. Yet it is the very fact that they lie so deeply buried that is problematic because we take them for granted and never consider them. The reality is that it is a useful exercise to examine what we believe and why we believe it.

Bitterness

Wouldn't our enemies rub their hands with glee if they knew that our hate for them was exhausting us, making us tired and nervous, ruining our looks, giving us heart trouble, and probably shortening our lives? *Dale Carnegie*

Heat not a furnace for your foe so hot it do singe yourself. *William Shakespeare*

Get rid of all bitterness, rage and anger, brawling and slander, along with every form of malice. Be kind and compassionate to one another, forgiving each other. *The Bible – Ephesians 4:31–32*

Bitterness

A lot of things in life have the potential to make us bitter, but no matter how long we nurse a grudge, it won't get better. Have you ever had a problem with a persistent weed that grew rapidly and pushed up its ugly stalk and leaves? Have you ever tried chopping it down, hoping to discourage it from coming back, but it kept coming back? Only after removing the root can the problem be solved. Roots of bitterness can go very deep into our lives so that periodic pruning will not solve the problem. Only the major surgery of forgiveness will get out the root cause.

Business

Always remember that this whole thing started with a mouse. *Walt Disney*

You never get a second chance to make a good first impression. *Will Rogers*

It isn't the number of people employed in a business that makes it successful, it's the number working. If your business keeps you so busy that you have no time for anything else, there must be something wrong, either with you or with your business. *William Boetcker*

It's been said that the six most important words in communications and human relations are: 'I admit that I was wrong.' The five most important words are: 'You did a great job.' The four most important words are: 'What do you think?' The three most important words are: 'May I help?' The two most important words are: 'Thank you.' The most important word is 'we' and the least important word is 'I'.

Busyness

The really idle man gets nowhere. The perpetually
busy man does not get much further.
Sir Heneage Ogilvie

We all have times when we have to be busy. Busyness goes further: busyness is the way of life when you are permanently busy. Busyness used to be something that a few people suffered from; it has now become something that is almost compulsory. For example, within recent memory, travelling used to mean an enforced break from work; now the mobile phone and the notebook computer ensure that we can work wherever we are. And because we can, we do. Busyness is addictive. It can give an adrenaline rush that feels satisfying and it can (often on very little evidence) give a sense of achievement. Yet busyness is dangerous. It allows us to mistake activity for achievement and to think that, because we are busy, we are doing something useful. It can also erode the truly important things in life: our relationships with family, friends and God.

Certainty

Nothing is certain but death and taxes.
Benjamin Franklin

It is not certain that everything is uncertain.
Blaise Pascal

What men really want is not knowledge but certainty. *Bertrand Russell*

Do not expect to arrive at certainty in every subject, which you pursue. There are a hundred things wherein we mortals must be content with probability, where our best light and reasoning will reach no farther. *Isaac Watts*

What we believe is important, yet not all of our beliefs can be proved. Ironically, it seems that the more important a belief is, the harder it is to prove. For instance, it is easy enough to prove – or disprove – a belief that the car is locked or the washing has been done, but these are hardly life-changing matters. Yet if we think of some really important belief such as 'My wife/husband loves me', 'My job is fulfilling' or 'Life is good', we find that they are impossible to prove.

Ultimately (and rather extraordinarily) it is impossible to prove anything worth proving. We have to be content that total certainty in the most important matters of life is often going to be lacking.

So what must we do? The answer is that we need to recognise the point where there is enough data to provide an adequate basis for action. To sit around waiting for some final proof may well be to ensure that the train of life will leave the station without us.

Chance

I do not believe in a fate that falls on men however they act; but I do believe in a fate that falls on men unless they act. *G. K. Chesterton*

Destiny is simply having the vision to realise your dreams and the perseverance to keep working towards them. *C. Phillips*

God does not play dice with the universe. *Albert Einstein*

The cards you hold in the game of life mean very little – it's the way you play them that counts.

Increasingly, people talk about chance, destiny or fate ruling their lives. One result is that when events turn out against them, it is these mysterious forces that are to blame. Such views can be convenient excuses for failure. So when reviewing some failed business idea someone may simply say, 'It wasn't meant to be,' instead of asking hard questions about why it failed.

There are other objections to these beliefs in chance, destiny and fate. First, the view that the ultimate control of our lives is totally beyond us is a deadly one. It has an anaesthetic effect, curbing initiative and discouraging hard work, sending us sleepwalking into the future. After all, why bother working, if our success or failure is ultimately determined by fate or destiny? Second, it dethrones God the Creator. To replace a loving and all-seeing God with a chance or destiny that is heartless and blind is to make the very worst of exchanges.

Change

Change is the law of life, and those who look only to the past or the present are certain to miss the future. *John F. Kennedy*

If your horse is dead, for goodness sake – dismount. *Eddy Ketchursid*

One change makes way for the next, giving us the opportunity to grow. *Vivien Buchen*

If you board the wrong train, it is no use running along the corridor in the other direction. *Dietrich Bonhoeffer*

Change

Life is always at some turning point. Everything flows; nothing stays still. Change is not something to be feared, it is something we should welcome.

There are three common traps that keep us from recognising and using change:

1. Believing that yesterday's solutions solve today's problems.
2. Assuming present trends will always continue.
3. Ignoring the opportunities created by future change.

Don't get trapped in the past, believing that change is an enemy. Welcome change as a friend.

The hardest thing to change is our attitude to change. Expect change. It is inevitable. Our decision is to decide whether it is by consent or coercion.

Two caterpillars were crawling across the grass when a butterfly flew over them. They looked up and one said to the other: 'You will never get me up in one of those.'

Character

In the last analysis, what we are communicates far
more eloquently than anything we say or do.
Stephen Covey

You cannot dream yourself into a character; you
must hammer and forge yourself one.
James A. Froude

In matters of style, swim with the current; in matters
of principle, stand like a rock. **Thomas Jefferson**

Character is a long-standing habit. **Plutarch**

What is character? Character is the shorthand word for how reliable, honest, courageous and caring we really are. It is the sum of our internal qualities. Character is much easier kept than recovered. Character is of great importance, because it controls how we live our lives and what, in any particular situation, we are likely to do. A good way to judge someone's character is by observing how they treat those who cannot offer them anything.

Sadly, the idea of character is little understood today. It seems to be assumed that what we are is the product of things that are outside our control, notably our genes and our upbringing. Yet, in reality, character is different. Good character is not a gift; it is something that we must choose to build for ourselves. Every choice we make, to do right or wrong, to be courageous or cowardly, to struggle or to give in, goes towards building up or tearing down our characters.

Ultimately, our characters matter, because it is our characters, and not our achievements, that will determine our true value. Have character – don't just be one!

Choices

There is a time when we must firmly choose the
course we will follow, or the relentless drift of
events will make a decision.
Herbert V. Prochnow

You are free to choose, but the choices you make
today will determine what you will have, be, and do
in the tomorrow of your life. *Zig Ziglar*

Every single day we make choices that show
whether we are courageous or cowardly. We
choose between the right thing and the convenient
thing, sticking to a conviction or caving in for the
sake of comfort, greed or approval. *Bill Hybels*

Your capacity to say 'No' determines your capacity
to say 'Yes' to greater things. *E. Stanley Jones*

Choices

In the film *Groundhog Day* actor Bill Murray wakes up to the same day over and over again. He finds himself confronted with the same situations he had faced just the day before all over again, only of course it isn't a new day – he's stuck on Groundhog Day. Only he is aware of the repetition that is taking place as he experiences the events of the day before. Confronted with the same choices once again, Murray is able to change what had happened previously by making a different choice.

Let us learn from poor choices by making wiser ones today. The doors we open and close each day decide the lives we live.

Commitment

Commitment is the enemy of resistance, for it is the serious promise to press on, to get up, no matter how many times you are knocked down.
David McNally

I offer neither pay, or quarters, nor provisions; I offer hunger, thirst, forced marches, battles and death. Let him who loves his country with his heart and not with his lips only, follow me! *Giuseppe Garibaldi*

Whatever I have tried to do in life, I have tried with all my heart to do it well. Whatever I have devoted myself to, I have devoted myself to completely.
Charles Dickens

Commitment unlocks the doors of imagination, allows vision, and gives us the 'right stuff' to turn our dreams into reality. *James Womack*

It might be possible to make a car where all the parts were held together simply by gravity or friction. Such a vehicle would not, of course, travel far and would fall apart at the first bump. Clearly, any working vehicle must be assembled using secure fastenings such as nuts and bolts. In human society, commitment takes the role of the nuts and bolts; it bonds words and promises into actions. Without commitment, life would be full of empty statements of intent that went no further than words.

Commitment involves two things. First, commitment accepts the possibility of a cost. There can be no such thing as a cost-less or a risk-free commitment; to be committed to someone or something is to say: 'For better or worse, come what may, I am committed to you.' Second, commitment rejects the possibility of running away. To be committed to someone or something is to bind your future with theirs until the task agreed is completed. It may even be an open-ended commitment with no expiry date. To make a commitment is both to make a promise and to be faithful to that promise. A commitment is doing what you said you would do long after the feeling you had when you said it has passed!

Yet if the cost of commitment is high, so are its rewards. Without commitment very little that will last can be achieved. With commitment, extraordinary ventures can be both dared and accomplished.

A chicken and a pig were talking in a field, when a bus went past with a poster 'Egg and bacon – the great British breakfast'. The chicken said to the pig, 'Look at that bus! They are talking about us.' The pig replied, 'It's all right for you, you only have to make a contribution. For me it costs me my life!'

Communication

The real art of conversation is not only to say the right thing in the right place, but to leave unsaid the wrong thing at the tempting moment.
Dorothy Nevill

The two words information and communication are often used interchangeably, but they signify quite different things. Information is giving out; communication is getting through.
Sydney J. Harris

There may be no single thing more important in our efforts to meaningful work and fulfilling relationships than to learn the art of communication. *Max De Pree*

Communication does not begin with being understood; but with understanding others.
Steven Brown

A message sent is only as good as the receiver's perception of it. The word 'communication' is derived from the Latin word *communicare* which means 'held in common'. For effective communication, we have to make sure that the people we are communicating with understand what we are saying.

In an old fable, the sun and the wind had a contest to see who could get a man to take his coat off. The wind blew harder and harder, and the man only drew his coat closer around him. Then the sun sent out its warmth, and in a short time the man willingly took off his coat. Some communication is like a cold wind to the hearers. It makes them defensive. But, when our speaking is warm, understanding and relevant, then our communication is effective. Let's say what we mean and mean what we say, but don't say it mean.

Compassion

If we could only read the secret history of our enemies, we would find in each man's life sorrow and suffering enough to disarm all hostility.
Henry Wadsworth Longfellow

How far you go in life, depends on your being tender with the young, compassionate with the aged, sympathetic with the striving, and tolerant of the weak and the strong. Because someday in life, you will have been all of these.
George Washington Carver

Everybody wants to right the world; nobody wants to help their neighbour. *Henry Miller*

The people who work in an Intensive Care Unit in a hospital can't seem to do enough for those in need. Everyone is caring and thoughtful. The distinctions of race and class melt away. Each person pulls together for everyone else. The world changes in an Intensive Care Unit.

Why? Because people know that loving and caring for someone else is what life is really about. If we lived our lives as people working in an Intensive Care Unit maybe more compassion would flow.

I like the story of a school class that had fourteen ten-year-old boys who had no hair. Only one, however, had no choice in the matter. Ian O'Gorman was undergoing chemotherapy for lymphoma and his hair was falling out so he had his head shaved. But then thirteen of his classmates shaved their heads so Ian wouldn't feel out of place.

Kindness will influence more than eloquence. We are not here on earth to see through one another, but to see one another through. We grow in our maturity when we sense our concern for others outweighing our concern for ourselves.

Imagine you are in an Intensive Care Unit. Who needs compassion in your life right now?

Conscience

Conscience is the still small voice that makes you
feel still smaller. *Anon*

A good conscience is a continual feast.
Robert Burton

A lot of people mistake a short memory for a clear
conscience. *Doug Larson*

Living with a conscience is like driving a car with the brakes on. Conscience is that inner sense that tells us whether what we are doing – or plan to do – is right or wrong. Conscience is the alarm that is triggered whenever we consider wrong actions. Conscience is something inside that bothers you when nothing outside does. A guilty conscience never thinks itself safe. To have a good conscience is to know serenity and that you are living up to your own standards.

Yet the conscience is the most vulnerable of things. It can be ignored and, if so treated, will eventually wither away so that it stays silent during even the most evil acts. It can also be distorted so that it approves what is wrong and condemns what is right. Conscience is like a delicate stringed instrument that frequently gets out of tune and has to be re-tuned. Conscience, like a pencil, needs to be sharpened occasionally.

So how do we tune our consciences? The answer is that we need to regularly set them alongside the finest standard that we can find and ask ourselves: 'What would he or she do under these circumstances?' The highest and most accurate standard that we can tune our consciences to is that of Jesus. If we are conscious of a bad conscience, it's wise to deal with it. The beginning of honesty is the confession of dishonesty. A clear conscience smiles at false accusations.

Contentment

To secure a contented spirit, measure your desires
by your fortune, and not your fortune by your
desires. *Jeremy Taylor*

Content makes poor men rich. Discontent makes
rich men poor. *Benjamin . Franklin*

We may pass violets looking for roses. We may pass
contentment looking for victory. *Bern Williams*

I have learned in whatever state I am, to be content.
St Paul

Better a little, with content, than much with
contention. *Anon*

There are two ways to get enough: one is to
continue to accumulate more and more. The other
is to desire less. *G. K. Chesterton*

The grass, as we know, always appears greener on the other side of the fence. People live in one of two tents: content or discontent. However long you take agonising over the menu deciding which dessert to have, when the person's next to you arrives you realise you have made the wrong choice. God made us a little lower than the angels, but most of us are concerned to climb a little higher than the Joneses.

The average family ambition is to make as much money as they are spending. But our yearnings will always exceed our earnings. Just when we think we are going to make ends meet, someone moves the ends. A story is told of a king who was suffering from anxiety and discontentment. He was advised that he would be cured if the shirt of a contented man was brought for him to wear. People went out to all parts of the kingdom after such a person, and after a long search they found a man who was really happy and content. But he did not own a shirt.

In Charles Dickens *A Christmas Carol* Old Marley's ghost lamented a life of clinging to money: 'my Spirit never roved beyond the narrow limits of our money changing hole'.

Two and a half thousand years earlier, the writer

of the book of Ecclesiastes knew this only too well: 'Those who love money will never have enough. How meaningless to think that wealth brings true happiness' (The Bible, New Living Translation – Ecclesiastes 5:10).

We lose our health to make money and then we lose our money to find health.

If you cannot have everything, make the best of everything you have. The best way to have a contented state of mind is to count our blessings not our cash. We need to be content while having ambitions and goals.

A farmer lived on the same farm all his life. It was a good farm, but with the passing of years the farmer began to tire and longed for a change, for something better. Every day he found a new reason for criticising some feature of the farm. Finally, he decided to sell and contacted an agent, who prepared a sale advertisement. As one might expect, it emphasised all the farm's advantages – ideal location, modern equipment, healthy stock, acres of fertile ground. Before advertising, the agent called the farmer and read the copy to him for his approval. When he'd finished, the farmer said, 'Hold everything. I've changed my mind. I'm not going to sell. I've been looking for a place like that all my life'!

Do you have an attitude of gratitude? A man had no shoes and complained until he met a man who had no feet.

Let's be grateful for what we already have. True contentment is found not in having everything you want, but in not wanting to have everything.

Courage

Courage is not the absence of fear; rather it is the ability to take action in the face of fear.
Nancy Anderson

All our dreams can come true — if we have the courage to pursue them. *Walt Disney*

Courage is doing what you are afraid to do. There can be no courage unless you are afraid.
Eddie Rickenbacker

One of the most moving passages in English literature comes towards the end of Charles Dickens *A Tale of Two Cities*, a story of the French Revolution.

Each day, a grim procession of prisoners made their way through the streets of Paris to the guillotine. One prisoner, Sidney Carton, a brave man who had once lost his soul but had found it again, was now giving his life for his friend. Beside him there was a young girl. They had met before in the prison, and the girl had noticed the man's gentleness and courage. She said to him: 'If I may ride with you, will you let me hold your hand? I am not afraid, but I am little and weak, and it will give me more courage.'

So they rode together, her hand in his, and when they reached the place of execution, there was no fear in her eyes. She looked up into the quiet composed face of her companion and said: 'I think you were sent to me by heaven.'

In all the dark valleys of life, let us be courageous and let us encourage others on the journey.

Creativity

Capital isn't so important in business. Experience isn't so important. You can get both these things. What is important is ideas. If you have ideas, you have the main asset you need, and there isn't any limit to what you can do with your business and your life. *Harvey Firestone*

The Creative Dilemma: Every valuable creative idea will always be logical in hindsight. *Willis Harmon*

Creativity is allowing yourself to make mistakes. Art is knowing which ones to keep. *Scott Adams*

Creativity

Creativity is not as honoured as it ought to be. It is seen as a threat both by cynics who sneer that nothing will change and by conformists who command that nothing must change. And because creativity is a delicate flower that needs light, space and encouragement it is all too easily suffocated.

Yet there are at least two good reasons why we should encourage creativity. The first is this: the opening page of the Bible, which tells how God created the universe, also states that human beings are made in God's image. Being creative must therefore be part of what it means to be human. The second reason is much more down-to-earth. The history of the human race is largely that of creativity: without creativity we would still be wearing skins and shivering in caves. The mind once stretched by a new idea can never return to its original dimensions.

D

Death

I am dying as I have lived, beyond my means.
Oscar Wilde

When good men die, their goodness does not
perish. *Euripides*

I am ready to meet my maker. Whether my Maker
is prepared for the ordeal of meeting me is another
matter. *Winston Churchill*

I'm not afraid to die. I just don't want to be there
when it happens. *Woody Allen*

As a well-spent day brings happy sleep, so a life well
spent brings happy death. *Leonardo da Vinci*

Louis XV, King of France, was so afraid of death that he ordered that the subject was never to be spoken of in his presence. Nothing that could in any way remind him of death was to be mentioned or displayed, and he sought to avoid every place, sign and monument which, in any way, suggested death. But, despite his efforts, death eventually met up with him.

Many people seem to imitate King Louis and prefer to avoid thinking about death. Yet while to think of death may be sad, to ignore it is folly. The fact of death challenges many of our beliefs. For one thing, recognising that one day we will all depart this life with nothing sheds a much-needed light on our culture's obsession with possessions. For another, death rebukes our desire for power and status; in the grave all are equal.

But can we look death in the face? Over the centuries there are many that have found comfort in Jesus' words: 'I am the resurrection and the life. Anyone who believes in me will live, even though they die; and whoever lives by believing in me will never die' (The Bible, Today's New International Version – John 11:25–26).

No greater words of hope exist. If they are true then the grave is not an ending; it is a new beginning.

Determination

Be like a postage stamp. Stick to something until you get there. *Josh Billings*

We can learn to soar, only in direct proportion to our determination to rise above the doubt and transcend the limitations. *David McNally*

Never give in! Never give in! Never, never, never. Never – in anything great or small – never give in except to convictions of honour and good sense. *Winston Churchill*

I am only one, but I am one. I cannot do everything, but I can do something; and what I can do, that I ought to do; and what I ought to do, by the grace of God I shall do. *Edward Hale*

Florence Nightingale accepted the challenge to upgrade hospital standards, improving patient care, enhancing sanitation and promoting nursing education. The determination of one woman transformed hospitals from a place where people die, to a place of healing and hope.

During the Crimean War she rose by 4.30 a.m. to leave for the battlefields where inferior medical care caused British soldiers to die unnecessarily. After incredible exploits, saving lives with her team of nurses, Nightingale returned to England.

Confined to her sick bed, she managed to establish, at the age of 40, the Nightingale School and Home for Nurses in London. She created a medical revolution from her bed and continued to direct initiatives till she died at the age of 90.

Despite the difficulties and challenges that Florence Nightingale endured, her determination and endurance eased the pain and discomfort of thousands.

Dreams

Hold fast to dreams, for if dreams die,
Life is a broken-winged bird that cannot fly.
Hold fast to dreams, for when dreams go,
Life is a barren field frozen with snow.
Langston Hughes

Since it doesn't cost anything to dream, you'll never
short-change yourself, when you stretch your
imagination. *Robert Schuller*

The key is to have a dream that inspires us to go
beyond our limits. *Robert Kriegel*

When a dream takes hold of you, what can you do?
You can run with it, let it run your life, or let it go
and think for the rest of your life about what might
have been. *Patch Adams*

The path of dreamers usually follows a similar pattern. Their dreams are not generally accepted for some time. But it doesn't stop the dreamer. Henry Ford had a dream that grew out of his interest in mechanical things as a boy. He was intrigued by the automobile and built his first one in a shed behind his house. His dream was to put the horseless carriage, at that time only available to the wealthy, into the hands of everyone. He helped form the Detroit Motor Company, where his colleagues laughed at the idea of manufacturing their product inexpensively in order to sell to the masses. Ford left the company but he did not leave his dream.

In 1903 he established the Ford Motor Company and produced the Model T. The first year, only 6,000 cars were built, but only eight years later, over 500,000 cars a year rolled off the line. They were able to reduce the cost from $850 to $360. Ford's dream had come to pass. Following our dream, we begin to see ourselves in a new light, having greater potential and capable of stretching and growing to reach our dream so that every opportunity we meet, every resource we discover, every talent we develop, becomes a part of our potential to grow towards that dream. A dream provides a reason to go, a path to follow and a target to hit.

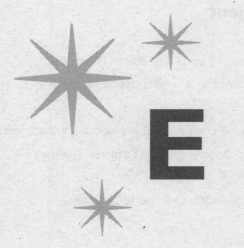

E

Encouragement

People do not live by bread alone. They need buttering up once in a while. *Robert Henry*

When someone does something good, applaud! You will make two people happy. *Samuel Goldwyn*

Silent gratitude isn't much use to anyone.
G. B. Stern

Encouragement

Research has shown that for every critical comment we receive, it takes nine affirming comments to even out the negative effect in our life. The word encouragement means 'to put courage into'. Encouragement is like oxygen to the soul. Encouragement is needed to face day-to-day challenges.

A smile of encouragement at the right moment may act like sunlight on a closed up flower; it may be the turning point for a struggling life. Few things in the world are more powerful than a positive lift, a smile, a word of optimism and hope, a 'You are doing well' and a 'You can do it' when things are tough. Reach down and lift someone up. It's a healthy exercise.

Enthusiasm

Enthusiasm is the sparkle in your eyes; it is the grip of your hand, the irresistible surge of your will, and your energy to execute your ideas.
Henry Ford

What I do best is share my enthusiasm.
Bill Gates

Success is going from failure to failure without loss of enthusiasm. *Winston Churchill*

We can succeed at almost anything for which we have unlimited enthusiasm.
Andrew Carnegie

Enthusiasm is one of the most important ingredients in life. Nothing is as contagious as enthusiasm and nothing great was ever achieved without enthusiasm. The word 'enthusiasm' is derived from the Greek word *entheos*, which means 'God within'.

Enthusiastic people are people who make a difference because their inner being has been ignited. Enthusiasm is faith in action. Enthusiasm is not contrary to reason – it is reason on fire. We can't captivate other people if we haven't been captivated ourselves. The task to which you dedicate yourself can never become drudgery. Make sure that what you aspire to accomplish is worth accomplishing, and then put your heart into it. It is a mark of wisdom, no matter what we are doing, to have a good time doing it. Each day is filled with countless opportunities that are waiting to be grasped by those who are enthusiastic.

Example

We must be the change we wish to see in the world. *Mahatma Gandhi*

Setting an example is not the main means of influencing another. It is the only means.
Albert Einstein

Be such a person, and live such a life, that if every person were such as you, and every life a life such as yours, this earth would be God's paradise.
Phillips Brooks

Example

One day, St Francis of Assisi invited a young monk to join him on a trip to a local village to preach. The young novice, delighted to be singled out to be Francis' companion, accepted with enthusiasm. They walked through the main streets, turned down many of the alleys, made their way into the suburbs and then returned to the monastery. As they returned, the young novice monk reminded Francis of the original intention: 'You have forgotten, Father, that we went to the town to preach.'

'My son,' Francis replied, 'we have preached. We were preaching while we were walking. We have been seen by so many, our behaviour has been closely watched; it was thus that we preached our morning sermon. It is of no use to walk anywhere to preach, unless we preach everywhere as we walk.'

We can preach a better sermon with our lives than with our lips. It is true that when we walk the talk, people listen. The best testament is the living testament.

Excellence

There is none who cannot teach somebody something, and there is none so excellent that they cannot be excelled. *Baltasar Gracián*

Real excellence does not come cheaply. A certain price must be paid in terms of practice, patience and persistence. *Stephen Covey*

Excellence is to do a common thing in an uncommon way. *Booker T. Washington*

Former US Secretary of State, Henry Kissinger, asked an aide to write a report. The aide researched and wrote the report. After receiving the report, Henry Kissinger sent it back to the aide with a note: 'Redo it.' The aide diligently reworked the report and gave it in, only to be told to redo it again. After the third time the aide asked to see Henry Kissinger. 'I have completed this report three times,' he said, 'and this is the best job I can do.'

Henry Kissinger replied, 'In that case, I'll read your report now.'

Often, the greatest enemy of excellence is just 'good'. If we refuse to accept anything but the very best, we will often get it.

Excellence is an attitude that motivates us to go beyond the normal call of duty. It's looking at the bigger picture, but not ignoring the details and being willing to go the extra mile. Excellence is not a matter of chance, it's a matter of choice.

Experience

Experience is a good school but the fees are high.
Heinrich Heine

Experience is not what happens to you, it is what you do with what happens to you.
Aldous Huxley

Experience is a hard teacher because she gives the test first, the lesson afterwards. *Vernon Law*

What we have to learn to do, we learn by doing.
Aristotle

Experience is the name that everyone gives to their mistakes. *Oscar Wilde*

Experience

There are very few advantages of old age but experience is one of them. An older person may, on the basis of their experience, come to the right conclusion a long time before a much younger person, who has to work their way using first principles. Yet there are two cautions that need to be issued concerning experience.

The first caution is that experience is not something that is automatically gained with advancing years. Some people have a vast number of experiences but they never learn a thing from them. To get experience, you don't just need to have experiences; you need to be able to analyse what went wrong (or right) and learn from it. Experience is only a great teacher to those who are prepared to be taught. Experience makes us either better or bitter.

The second caution is that while experience is a useful basis for knowledge, it is limited. Experience can, by definition, only teach us about what we have already experienced; it has nothing to say about a new situation. Experience is a good basis for making a judgement, but it is no substitute for thinking. Listen to the voice of experience, but also make use of your brains.

F

Failure

Many of life's failures are people who did not realise
how close they were to success when they gave up.
Thomas Edison

Failure is the opportunity to begin again more
intelligently. *Henry Ford*

Success is never final; failure is never fatal; it is the
courage to continue that counts.
Winston Churchill

Failure

We have all failed many times. We fell down the first time we tried to walk. We thought we were drowning the first time we tried to swim. An essential part of creativity is not being afraid to fail. Scientists came up with wise words for their research: 'hypotheses' and 'experiments'.

Most successes have been built on failures. Henry Ford forgot to put a reverse gear in his first car. Many of the great accomplishments in history have been the result of persistent perseverance against failure and disappointment. Our failings can often be a vital ingredient to our success. A teacher at Harrow School wrote on the sixteen-year-old Winston Churchill's report card: 'A conspicuous lack of success.' It's a good job that Winston Churchill didn't take any notice! Failure should be a wise teacher, a temporary detour, not a dead-end. We will frequently fail, but if we are to succeed, we must rise each time we fall. Failure is staying there on the floor.

Faith

In actual life every great enterprise begins with and takes its first forward step in faith.
Friedrich von Schlegel

Now faith is the substance of things hoped for, the evidence of things not seen.
The Bible, New King James Version –
Hebrews 11:1

Faith is to believe what you do not see; the reward of this faith is to see what you believe.
St Augustine

Faith is like a muscle which grows stronger and stronger with use, rather than rubber, which weakens when it is stretched. *J. O. Fraser*

Only those who believe are obedient. Only those who are obedient, believe. *Dietrich Bonhoeffer*

Faith is commonly seen as something that is entirely to do with the mind. Yet in reality, real faith is always linked to action. You can say, 'I believe that parachuting is safe' as frequently as you like but it is a statement that only really has any meaning when you do actually jump out of a plane with a parachute on your back. The fact is that most beliefs have implications attached. So, for example, to say, 'I believe this is a good investment' raises the question as to why you, personally, are not investing in it.

The fact that faith is inextricably linked with action explains a lot of unbelief. After all, if something is going to require that you do something about it, then it is far easier to pretend that it isn't true. Some people refuse to believe in God, not because of the facts but because of the implications. Yet to fail to believe because we dare not believe is hardly honest. Faith is a principle by which to live, not a problem to be solved. As a student I was an atheist and then I discovered that God doesn't believe in atheists!

Family

Perhaps the greatest social service that can be rendered by anybody to the country and to humankind is to bring up a family.
George Bernard Shaw

No matter how many communes anybody invents, the family always creeps back. *Margaret Mead*

The presidency is temporary, but the family is permanent. *Yvonne De Gaulle*

One of the great mysteries of life is how the idiot that your daughter married can be the father of the most beautiful and intelligent grandchildren in the world. *Anon*

All the wealth in the world cannot be compared with the happiness of living together happily united.
Margaret Youville

It is easy to be cynical about families, and never more so than in an age when many of us have experienced the disintegration of a family. Yet, as so often, cynicism steals more than it gives. What else is there to replace the family as the basis of social life and as the setting in which children are brought up? The 24-hour state nursery? The neighbourhood association? The collective farm? The fact is that when it comes to a basic social unit, the family – however flawed it may be in practice – is the best option. Our efforts need focussing not towards abolishing the idea of families but towards repairing and maintaining them.

Yet, as with so many things, it is easy to be dangerously long-sighted with the family: to focus on the general picture in the distance rather than on the specific issues at our feet. To save the family it is not enough for us to mutter approvingly about encouraging 'The Family'; we need to start with our own family. There are very few families that cannot benefit from such things as a get-together, a few phone calls, a shared meal. Like charity, improving the family should begin at home.

Fear

Often the fear of one evil leads us into a worse one. *Nicolas Boileau*

The only thing we have to fear is fear itself — nameless, unreasoning, unjustified terror which paralyses needed efforts to convert retreat into advance. *Franklin D. Roosevelt*

The wise man in the storm prays to God, not for safety from danger, but for deliverance from fear. It is the storm within that endangers him, not the storm without. *Ralph Waldo Emerson*

I am afraid of airplanes, deep-sea diving and psychiatry. The earth alone comforts me, regardless of how much dirt it may contain.
Françoise Sagan

Fear

The problem with fear is not fear itself but what fear produces in us. Although fear is no more than an extremely unpleasant emotion, it can be enormously destructive. Fear is that little dark room where negatives are developed.

First of all, fear prevents good being done. Out of fear, people refuse to take up challenges, avoid performing acts of kindness and avoid situations where they might be able to help. Fear makes us selfish, cautious and cowardly. Second, fear encourages evil. Fear can turn good men and women into the voiceless bystanders of evil acts.

We cannot escape fear, so let us transform it and instead of allowing us to anticipate the worst, let us imagine the best that can happen.

Focus

If you chase two rabbits, both will escape. *Anon*

Here is the prime condition of success: Concentrate your energy, thought and capital exclusively upon the business in which you are engaged. Having begun on one line, resolve to fight it out on that line, to lead in it, adopt every improvement, have the best machinery, and know the most about it.
Andrew Carnegie

We tell children off for taking more food on their plates than they can eat. Adults, however, are often guilty of the same offence with regard to life. In the past the options faced by a man or woman were limited. He could take his father's trade or starve; she could do housework at home or get married and do the housework elsewhere. Now, we have an almost infinite number of choices for work and leisure and the access to knowledge has never been so easy or so cheap. The result, though, has not been the production of experts and excellence; it has instead been vast numbers of people who know a little about a lot. We have traded depth for shallowness.

The fact is that for excellence in any area, whether it be in a career, in business, in the arts or in a sport, focus is needed. Focus is the ability to define a single goal, to concentrate your energies on achieving it and to refuse to be side-tracked by anything else. Without focus, almost nothing that is of lasting value is ever produced.

Forgiveness

Forgiveness is the fragrance the violet sheds on the heel that has crushed it. *Mark Twain*

Never does the human soul appear so strong and noble as when it forgoes revenge and dares to forgive an injury. *E. H. Chapin*

'I can forgive, but I cannot forget' is only another way of saying, 'I will not forgive.'
Henry Ward Beecher

Forgiveness

The Lord's Prayer, which Jesus taught, asks God to 'Forgive us our trespasses, as we forgive those who trespass against us'. If we are not prepared to forgive other people, we should not expect God to forgive us.

We must learn to forgive because resentments are heavy burdens we don't need to carry. Without forgiveness our lives are driven by bitterness and this imprisons us. We need to forgive our family, friends and foes. In the words of Francis of Assisi, 'It is in pardoning that we are pardoned.'

Forgiveness doesn't make the other person right, it liberates us. Forgiving other people is one of the greatest proofs of our love. It is wiser to forgive and forget than it is to hate and remember. The practice of forgiveness is our most important contribution to the healing of our relationships and, therefore, to the healing and liberation of humankind.

Freedom

People hardly ever make use of the freedom they
have, for example, freedom of thought; instead they
demand freedom of speech as a compensation.
Søren Kierkegaard

Give me the liberty to know, to utter, and to argue
freely according to conscience, above all liberties.
John Milton

The right to be heard does not automatically
include the right to be taken seriously.
Hubert Humphrey

Liberty without obedience is confusion and
obedience without liberty is slavery.
William Penn

Freedom is not constituted primarily of privileges
but of responsibilities. *Albert Camus*

Freedom is held to be one of the greatest of all virtues. Men and women die for it, poems and songs are written about it, festivals commemorate it. The focus of our attention is, however, always on external, political freedom; we overlook the fact that, even in a free society, lives can be in chains. Everywhere we find people who are enslaved to prejudices, imprisoned by fears, handcuffed by their beliefs and trapped by their desires. The tragedy is that many who seem free are in fact enslaved and their slavery may be so subtle and deep-rooted that they do not realise that they are not free.

In the private world of our minds and thoughts, liberation is far harder. Freedom here is more precious; someone physically in chains may retain some mental freedom but none whose mind is enslaved can possess any sort of freedom. It is this sort of deep personal freedom that Jesus talked about when he said to those who followed him, 'You will know the truth and the truth will set you free.' The first two steps to deep and real freedom are to come to know the truth of what enslaves us and to discover Jesus, who can really free us.

Friendship

Friendship is the inexpressible comfort of feeling
safe with a person, having neither to weigh thoughts
nor measure words. *George Eliot*

My friends are the ones who bring out the best in
me. *Henry Ford*

You can make more friends in two months by
becoming interested in other people than you can
in two years by trying to get other people
interested in you. *Dale Carnegie*

Friendship

A king loved to disguise himself and mingle with his people. Once, dressed as a poor man, he descended the long flight of stairs, dark and damp, to the tiny cellar where the furnace keeper, seated on ashes, was tending the furnace. The king sat down beside him and began to talk. At mealtimes, the furnace keeper produced some coarse bread and a jug of water and they ate and drank. The king went away, but returned often for his heart was filled with compassion for the furnace keeper.

As time passed, they became very good friends. At last the king thought, 'I'll tell him who I am, and see what gift he will ask for.' So he did, but the furnace keeper didn't ask for a thing. The king was astonished and said, 'Don't you realise that I can give you anything – a city, a throne?' The man gently replied, 'I understand, Your Majesty. You have already given the greatest gift a man could receive. You left your palace to sit with me here in this dark and lonely place. You could give nothing more precious. You have given yourself and that is far more than I could ever deserve.'

Future

The future is not something we enter. The future is something we create. *Leonard Sweet*

There is nothing like a dream to create the future. *Victor Hugo*

If we open a quarrel between the past and the present, we shall find that we have lost the future. *Winston Churchill*

The future you shall know when it has come; before then, forget it. *Aeschylus*

I have long considered it one of God's greatest mercies that the future is hidden from us. If it weren't, life would surely be unbearable. *Eugene Forsey*

There are two common attitudes that people have towards the future. The first is fear: a dreaded certainty that what is going to happen is bound to be terrible. The future frightens some people, who prefer to live in the past. But those who fear the future are likely to fumble about in the present. The second is fatalism: the view – associated with the shrug of the shoulders – that the future is inevitable and that all we can do is bear it. Both views are problematic. Those who are fearful are generally so preoccupied with fleeing from the future that they do little about it. And those who are fatalistic do nothing either; to them the future is too fixed to change.

A third and better viewpoint on the future is that of faith. This is typified by the little saying: 'I do not know what the future holds, but I do know who holds the future.' That sort of faith both removes fear and gives energy for action. Don't be afraid to trust an unknown future to an all-knowing God. And we make our future by the best use of the present.

Generosity

Real generosity is doing something nice for someone who will never find it out.

Frank Clark

Generosity is widely praised. Yet it is questionable how much it is practised. In fact, a good deal of what is proclaimed to be generosity is nothing of the sort but is instead a cheap imitation of the real thing.

For instance, there is costless generosity, where someone gives away something that is of no real value to them. There is self-glorifying generosity: the giving that recovers its cost in terms of publicity. And there is generosity with strings attached: the gift that puts an obligation on the giver. It is open to question whether any of these is the genuine article.

In contrast, three things mark true generosity. It costs the giver, it is given discreetly and it is given freely without obligations. The rejected opportunity to give is a lost opportunity to receive.

In Charles Dickens' *A Christmas Carol*, Ebenezer Scrooge is portrayed as a mean, selfish, unhappy old man who is only interested in making money and serving his own needs. As the story unfolds, Scrooge has a revelation of his shortcomings and is transformed. He begins to laugh and play, share and help. He is liberated from a life of self-centredness and becomes generous and happy. You can give without loving, but you can't love without giving.

Goals

> We succeed only as we identify in life a single
> overriding objective and make all other
> considerations bend to that one objective.
> *Dwight D. Eisenhower*

> It is a mistake to look too far ahead. Only one link in
> the chain of destiny can be handled at a time.
> *Winston Churchill*

> If you want to be happy, set a goal that commands
> your thoughts, liberates your energy and inspires
> your hopes. *Andrew Carnegie*

Goals

It is good to be a go-getter. But it's wise to know what it is you want to go and get. It has been said that many people aim at nothing and hit it with precision. There are people who want to be everywhere at once, and they get nowhere. The distance a person goes is not as important as the direction.

It is good to have long-range goals to keep us from being frustrated by short-range disappointments. An obstacle is something you see when you take your eyes off the goal. And never look back, unless you are planning to go that way. Arriving at one goal is the starting point to another.

Gratitude

If you haven't all the things you want, be grateful for all you don't have that you don't want.
N. Marty Radcliff

The hardest arithmetic to master is that which enables us to count our blessings. *Eric Hoffer*

Gratitude

It is easy to assume that gratitude is no more than a social invention: the results of endless generations of children being taught to say, 'Thank you'. Yet there is far more to gratitude than this. To be grateful for some favour and to express it is to take the pleasure that we have had in receiving and to let a part of that return back to the giver.

Above all, though, gratitude is good for us. Gratitude, by focussing on what we have, rather than on what we do not have, creates a positive mental atmosphere. It is hard for any feelings of cynicism, bitterness and greed to flourish when gratitude is present. Were a survey done of grateful and ungrateful people we would no doubt find that those who were grateful were happier, better balanced and more content with life. Gratitude is good for us and we are wise to practise it.

H

Happiness

Men can only be happy when they do not assume that the object of life is happiness.
George Orwell

Happiness is a butterfly which, when pursued, is always just beyond your grasp, but which, if you will sit down quietly, may alight upon you.
Nathaniel Hawthorne

Those who are happiest are those who do the most for others. *Booker T. Washington*

The supreme happiness of life is the conviction that we are loved. *Victor Hugo*

The American Constitution famously defines basic human rights as 'life, liberty, and the pursuit of happiness'. But what is happiness? And how do you pursue happiness?

Ironically, you cannot pursue happiness directly. You either fail to find it or get side-tracked in pursuing pleasure, which is a very different thing. The reality is that happiness is the by-product of loving, being loved and doing what is good and right. In its most enduring and most unshakeable form, happiness is found in knowing God. And defined like that, to pursue happiness is indeed one of the great goals of human existence.

Honesty

To be persuasive we must be believable; to be believable we must be credible; to be credible we must be truthful. *Edward R. Murrow*

A liar needs a good memory. *Quintillian*

You can fool some of the people all of the time, and all of the people some of the time; but you can't fool all of the people all of the time.
Abraham Lincoln

One dentist said to me once, while holding a needle in his hand, 'You might feel a little sting. On the other hand, it might feel as though you've been kicked in the mouth by a mule.'

I must say, I did appreciate the honesty, and the fun of it eased the pain!

Honesty may be the best policy but it is a costly one. It leaves us vulnerable to others and it can be misunderstood as a sign of naivety or weakness. Yet honesty brings its rewards: a clear conscience and the liberating freedom of not having to try to remember to whom we told what lie.

Someone with a guilty conscience wrote to the Inland Revenue department: 'I am having trouble sleeping because of my conscience, please find enclosed £1000 – if this doesn't cure my insomnia, I'll send you the rest.'

Not only does honesty have its positive rewards when we make it our rule of life, but it also spares us the consequences of dishonesty. Those who are dishonest are unable to believe what they say to themselves and so they end up not knowing who they are.

The challenge for those of us who are parents, is

that we cannot lift our children to a higher level
than that on which we live ourselves.

Hope

Don't let our fears hold us back from pursuing our hopes. *John F. Kennedy*

When you say a situation or a person is hopeless, you are slamming the door in the face of God. *Charles L. Allen*

The natural flights of the human mind are not from pleasure to pleasure, but from hope to hope. *Samuel Johnson*

At a university, there was a piano teacher who was simply and affectionately known as 'Herman'. One evening at a university concert, a renowned pianist became ill while performing a very difficult piece. No sooner had the artist retired from the stage than Herman rose from his seat in the audience, walked onstage, sat down at the piano and with great mastery completed the performance.

When Herman was asked how he was able to perform such a demanding piece so beautifully without notice and with no rehearsal, he replied, 'In 1939 I was a budding young concert pianist. I was arrested and placed in a concentration camp. The future looked bleak, but I knew that in order to keep the flicker of hope alive, that I might someday play again, I needed to practise every day. I began by fingering a piece on my bare board bed late one night. The next night I added a second piece and soon I was running through my entire repertoire. I did this for five years. It so happens that the piece I played tonight at the concert hall was part of that repertoire. That constant practice is what kept my hope alive. Every day I renewed my hope that I would one day be able to play my music again on a real piano, and in freedom.'

Humility

It is no great thing to be humble, when you are brought low; but to be humble, when you are praised, is a great and rare attainment.
St Bernard of Clairvaux

Humility is like underwear – essential, but indecent if it shows. *Helen Neilson*

Let someone else blow your horn and the sound will carry twice as far. *Will Rogers*

I seem to have been only like a boy, playing on the seashore, and diverting myself in now and then finding a smoother pebble or a prettier shell than ordinary, whilst the great ocean of truth lay all undiscovered before me. *Isaac Newton*

Awareness of our limitations enhances humility. When Johann Sebastian Bach was praised for his wonderful skill as an organist, he replied with humility and wit: 'There is nothing very wonderful about it. You have only to hit the right notes at the right moment and the instrument does the rest.'

Humility is remaining teachable. Humility is elusive – the moment you think you have it, you have lost it. There is a story about two mountain goats who met each other on a narrow ledge, just wide enough for one of them to pass. On one side there was a sheer cliff, and on the other side a steep wall. The two were facing each other and it was impossible to turn or to back up. How did they solve their dilemma? One of them lay down on the trail and let the other literally walk over him and both were safe. A wise lesson from two goats!

Humour

A cheerful heart is good medicine.
The Bible — Proverbs 17:22

Good humour is one of the best articles of dress
one can wear in society.
William Makepeace Thackeray

Imagination was given to man to compensate for
what he is not. A sense of humour was provided to
console him for what he is. *Horace Walpole*

Humour is by far the most significant activity of the
human brain. *Edward de Bono*

It is essential that we have a good sense of humour as it is a basic survival tool. And it is even more essential that we can laugh at ourselves. Humour is to life what shock absorbers are to cars. Laughter is a therapeutic tranquilliser with no side effects. Good humour is a tonic for the mind, body and the soul. A good sense of humour helps us to tolerate the unpleasant, overcome the unexpected and outlast the unbearable. A good sense of humour definitely prevents a 'hardening of the attitudes'. Lighten up!

Initiative

If there is no wind, row. *Greek Proverb*

The world is divided into people who do things and people who get the credit. Try, if you can, to belong to the first class. There's far less competition.
Dwight Morrow

People are always blaming their circumstances for what they are. I don't believe in circumstances. The people who get on in this world are the people who get up and look for the circumstances they want, and, if they can't find them, make them.
Attributed to George Bernard Shaw

Initiative

At the entrance to one company is a sign that reads:
'If you are like a wheelbarrow – going no further
than you are pushed – you need not apply for work
here. In our endeavours we must always exhibit
personal initiative and be willing to go the second
mile.'

Someone said there are three types of people in
the world: those who do not know what is
happening; those who watch what is happening; and
those who make things happen. Wise people take
the initiative. They see a problem and act on it.
Let's get moving!

Integrity

Integrity without knowledge is weak and useless, and knowledge without integrity is dangerous and dreadful. *Samuel Johnson*

In matters of taste, swim with the current; in matters of principle, stand like a rock. *Thomas Jefferson*

The integrity of men is to be measured by their conduct, not by their professions. *Junius*

The following is on a church monument dated 1629:

Go placidly amid the noise and haste, and remember what peace there may be in silence. As far as possible, speak your truth quietly and clearly; be on good terms with all persons, even the dull and ignorant, they too have their story.

Avoid loud and aggressive persons, they are vexations to the spirit. If you compare yourself with others you may become vain and bitter, for always there will be greater and lesser persons than yourself. Enjoy your achievements as well as your plans. Keep interested in your own career, however humble; exercise caution in your business affairs, for the world is full of trickery. But let this not blind you to what virtue there is; many persons strive for high ideals and everywhere life is full of heroism.

Be yourself. Especially, do not feign affection. Neither be cynical about love, for, in the face of aridity and disenchantment, it is perennial as the grass. Take kindly the counsel of the years, gracefully surrendering the things of youth. Nurture strength of spirit, to shield you in sudden misfortune. But do not distress yourself with imaginings. Many fears are born of fatigue and loneliness. Beyond a wholesome discipline, be gentle with yourself.

Be at peace with God and, whatever your labours and aspirations in the noisy confusion of life, keep peace with your soul. With all its sham, drudgery and broken dreams, it is still a beautiful world.

J

Jealousy

Jealousy, the jaundice of the soul. *John Dryden*

The jealous are troublesome to others, but a torment to themselves. *William Penn*

The jealous and envious man feels others' fortunes are his misfortunes; their profit, his loss; their blessing, his bane; their health, his illness; their promotion, his demotion; their success, his failure. *Leslie Flynn*

Many lovely things pass out of life when jealousy
comes in. According to an ancient Greek legend, a
certain athlete ran well but came second in a race.
The winner was embraced with praise and
eventually a statue was erected in his honour.
Jealousy and envy ate away at the man who came
second. He resented the winner and he could think
of little else. Eventually he decided to destroy the
statue of the winner. Night after night, he went to
the statue under cover of darkness, chiselling away
at the base to weaken the foundation. But one night
as he chiselled, the heavy statue crashed down on
the disgruntled athlete. He died beneath the weight
of the marble replica of the man he had grown to
hate. His own jealousy and envy had destroyed him.

People can be jealous of another person's looks,
their way of life and their success. Jealousy is an
extraordinarily harmful attitude.

First, jealousy can ruin our own happiness. So,
for example, someone might be perfectly happy with
their own house until they see how much better
someone else's is. Second, jealousy ruins
thankfulness. Instead of having emotions of
gratitude we feel hurt and bitter. We are too busy

counting other people's blessings, rather than
counting our own.

Joy

Joy is the feeling of grinning inside.
Melba Colgrove

Joy is not a substitute for sex; sex is very often a
substitute for joy. I sometimes wonder whether all
pleasures are not substitutes for joy.
C. S. Lewis

Real joy comes not from ease or riches or from the
praise of others, but from doing something
worthwhile. *Wilfred Grenfell*

One of the things we envy children for is the ease with which they find joy. For many adults, joy is a stranger in their lives and they often cannot remember when they were last joyful. Indeed, it is easy to believe that joy is just one of those emotions that you experience when young and which, sadly, you grow out of with age.

But should this be the case? Should joy vanish with adolescence? It is striking that the Bible is full of instructions to rejoice. This seems to be a paradox; how can we work at what seems to be something that is entirely spontaneous? The answer lies in the fact that to rejoice (as to love) is both to feel an emotion and to act. Work at rejoicing by focussing your mind on the good things that there are in this world and you may come to experience joy. Focus your mind particularly on God, the maker of these good things, and the experience of joy is almost guaranteed.

Justice

If we do not maintain justice, justice will not maintain us. *Francis Bacon*

The sentiment of justice is so natural, and so universally acquired by all mankind, that it seems to be independent of all law, all party, all religion. *Voltaire*

Justice means to act in a way that is right, fair and impartial. It is to do the right thing, in the right way, with the right motives.

Justice is represented as being a blindfolded woman with scales and a sword – her scales are to weigh matters, her sword is to carry out judgement and her blindfold is to show that she is absolutely neutral. She can be trusted to be fair.

Acting justly is hard because it means considering other people's needs and, frequently, letting our own preferences and interests be pushed to one side. To act justly is to act. It is easy to speak a lot about justice, but actually to do very little. As the saying goes: 'Justice delayed is justice denied.'

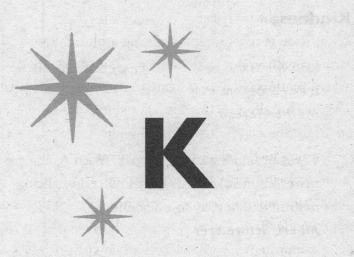

K

Kindness

Kind words can be short and easy to speak, but their echoes are truly endless.
Mother Teresa

Constant kindness can accomplish much. As the sun makes ice melt, kindness causes misunderstanding, mistrust and hostility to evaporate.
Albert Schweitzer

Kindness gives birth to kindness. *Sophocles*

Part of kindness is loving people more than they deserve. *Joseph Joubert*

In the film *Pay it Forward*, a reporter becomes the recipient of a random act of kindness after his car is smashed. The reporter is given a new car by a stranger, to replace his old wrecked car. He responds to the act of kindness by calling the stranger a freak because he cannot believe that someone would do this. He later learns that the man is returning the favour from another stranger who saved his daughter's life.

The man who saved his daughter's life told him: 'Pay it forward.' In other words, do three big random acts of kindness for three other strangers in need. He then instructs the reporter that he too must pay it forward. The concept of 'pay it forward' started from a classroom assignment in Social Studies where the teacher assigns his class the following task: 'Think of an idea to change our world and put it into action.'

An 11-year-old boy comes up with the idea. He tells his teacher that he did this, not for the grade, but because he really wanted to see if the world could and would change. The boy ends up losing his life when he tries to rescue a friend in trouble. But by the time he dies, his 'pay it forward' idea is in full motion across the country.

The man who gave the reporter the car had changed his thinking and therefore it affected his action of giving away the car. The reporter's thinking could not comprehend why anyone in their right mind would do anything like that. The reporter sets out to discover how this new thinking got started. He eventually traces it back to the boy. He discovered that his assignment, 'Think of an idea to change our world and put it into action,' has impacted and changed many lives.

L

Leadership

The first responsibility of a leader is to define reality.
The last is to say thank you. In between the leader is
a servant. *Max De Pree*

Reason and judgement are the qualities of a leader.
Tacitus

Leadership is the ability to get men to do what they
don't want to do and like it.
Harry S. Truman

A Leader

I went on a search to become a leader. I searched
high and low. I spoke with authority. People
listened. But alas, there was one who was wiser
than I, and they followed that individual. I sought to
inspire confidence, but the crowd responded, 'Why
should I trust you?'

I postured and I assumed the look of leadership
with a countenance that flowed with confidence
and pride. But many passed me by and never
noticed my air of elegance.

I ran ahead of the others; pointed the way to
new heights. I demonstrated that I knew the route
to greatness. And then I looked back and I was
alone.

'What shall I do?' I queried. 'I've tried hard and
used all I know.' And I sat down and pondered long.

And then I listened to the voices around me.
And I heard what the group was trying to
accomplish. I rolled up my sleeves and joined in the
work. As we worked, I asked: 'Are we all together in
what we want to do and how to get the job done?'

And we thought together, and we fought
together, and we struggled towards our goal. I found

myself encouraging the faint-hearted. I sought the ideas of those too shy to speak out. I taught those who had little skill. I praised those who worked hard. When our task was completed, one of the group turned to me and said, 'This would not have been done but for your leadership.'

At first, I said, 'I didn't lead, I just worked with the rest.' And then I understood leadership is not a goal. It's a way to reaching a goal. I lead best when I help others to use themselves creatively. I lead best when I forget about myself as leader. To lead is to serve, to give, to achieve together.

Anon

Learning

Value your listening and reading time at roughly ten times your talking time. This will assure you that you are on a course of continuous learning and self-improvement. *Gerald McGinnis*

Those who graduate today, and stop learning tomorrow, are uneducated the day after.
Newton Baker

I've never learned anything while I was talking.
Larry King

It's what you learn after you think you know it all that counts. *Kim Hubbard*

147

One of the problems of a formal educational system is the danger that, by the time we have finished school or college, we think that we have completed learning. The reality is otherwise; we must continue to learn all our lives. This has always been true but it is even more so in our times of unparalleled technological and cultural change.

Why do people stop learning? A large part of the answer lies in pride. To be proud is to have a mind so hardened by self-confidence that it sees no need to keep on learning. In contrast, humility encourages learning. To be humble is, in the best sense of the phrase, 'to have an open mind' and is the best frame of mind to approach new facts. Humility keeps us open to learning new things by reminding us that we really don't know very much.

Life

Life is like playing the violin solo in public and learning the instrument as you go.
Edward Bulwer-Lytton

Life is like an onion: you peel it off one layer at a time, and sometimes you weep.
Carl Sandburg

Our days on earth are as a shadow.
The Bible, New King James Version – 1 Chronicles 29:15

Life is what happens to you while you're making other plans. *William Gaddis*

To read any collection of modern quotations on the subject of life is to come face to face with bewilderment. Writer after writer expresses frustration and puzzlement over life and its meaning. Cyril Connolly is typical: 'Life is a maze in which we take the wrong turning before we have learnt to walk.' In this sea of bewildered frustration, about the only advice you can find is to make the most of life because it's over sooner than you think. Most people find this curiously unsatisfactory. Instinctively, we feel that life ought to have a meaning. We feel certain that somehow this whole extraordinary business of love, learning and loss ought to have some purpose and significance. To admit that all our struggles and labours are meaningless would make life the greatest and most widespread fraud ever perpetuated.

Here, as elsewhere, it seems far wiser to trust our instincts than our generation's gloomy guides. After all, just because someone has failed to find a meaning to life is not proof that there is no meaning. It may simply be that they were looking in the wrong place. Our life here on earth is a blip on the eternal screen. Let us live our lives in the light of eternity.

Loneliness

One may have a blazing hearth in one's soul, and yet no one ever comes to sit by it.
Vincent Van Gogh

It is strange to be known so universally and yet to be so lonely. *Albert Einstein*

There is no pleasure to me without communication: there is not so much as a sprightly thought comes into my mind that it does not grieve me to have produced alone, and that I have no one to tell it to.
Michel de Montaigne

Loneliness occurs in different forms. Being physically isolated is a fate that can either be inflicted on us by circumstances or one that is self-chosen. There can even be a mental loneliness that can afflict people who are surrounded by others.

However it occurs, loneliness is one of the saddest of conditions. Men and women are social beings; we are most fully alive when we are with other people. It is no accident that solitary confinement is the most dreaded form of imprisonment; fellowship with others can make even the worst circumstances bearable.

In no case is loneliness a good thing. We all need other people to encourage us, challenge our thinking, to correct us or to inspire us. Most of all, we need other people so that we have an opportunity to express kindness and love to someone.

We should do all we can to befriend those who are lonely. They need us.

Love

Love is the basic need of human nature, for without it life is disrupted emotionally, mentally, spiritually and physically. Love cures people – both the ones who give it and the ones who receive it.
Karl Menninger

What the world really needs is more love and less paperwork. *Pearl Bailey*

The first duty of love is to listen. *Paul Tillich*

What does 'love' mean? There is no more problematic word in the English language. We can say we 'would love' something when we mean that we would like it; we talk about 'falling in love' (which makes it sound like an irresistible emotion) and yet we make promises 'to love someone' (which makes it sound like a choice).

The answer is that there are several different but related and overlapping forms of love. But the greatest form of love does not centre on having affectionate feelings; it is rather to have a determined desire for good to occur to some other person. It is to make a decision to do good to them and to show kindness to them. Although this may sound much less dramatic than falling in love, it is of greater value. It can also be guaranteed, which is more than anything based on a feeling can be. Fortunately, when the Bible talks about God loving us it is this sort of love that is referred to. It is good to know that God's care for us rests on his promises, not just his feelings.

St Augustine wrote: 'God loves each one of us, as if there were only one of us.'

Loyalty

When we are debating an issue, loyalty means giving
me your honest opinion, whether you think I'll like it
or not. Disagreement, at this state, stimulates me.
But once a decision is made, the debate ends. From
that point on, loyalty means executing the decision
as if it were your own. *Colin Powell*

Lack of loyalty is one of the major causes of failure
in every walk of life. *Napoleon Hill*

Stand with anybody that stands right, stand with him
while he is right and part with him when he goes
wrong. *Abraham Lincoln*

We all like loyalty; especially when it is directed towards us. Loyalty is essential in many areas. Businesses with disloyal employees, marriages with disloyal spouses and armies with disloyal soldiers are not likely to last long. Yet loyalty is one of those things that needs handling carefully. Loyalty has its perils and unconditional loyalty in particular is very dangerous. To say, 'My country (or my company) is right (or wrong)' is to put loyalty above morality and opens the way to wrong acts, both great and small. Unconditional loyalty makes a 'god' out of whatever it is we pledge loyalty to. The best attitude to loyalty is to make sure that only God gets our unconditional loyalty and that he gets it always. With that as a safeguard we can afford to give our loyalty to other causes and other people.

Manners

The hardest job kids face today is learning good manners without seeing any. *Fred Astaire*

Protocol is everything. *Francois Giuliani*

It is easy to mock manners. You can mock them as being entirely a product of social convention. You can also mock them on the basis that many a crook has been hidden beneath a mask of good manners. Both criticisms have some foundation. Yet manners should not be totally dismissed. For one thing, to ignore manners is – as someone has said – 'to throw sand into the delicate machinery of society'; everything becomes harder and more painful. For another, although manners and morals may often have only a limited connection, there is a link. To have love for other people is, at its most basic level, to care for them; so to have good manners in order that someone feels comfortable is to take the first step on the ladder of love. It may be the lowest step, but it is a step nonetheless.

Marriage

To keep your marriage brimming
With love in your loving cup,
Whenever you're wrong admit it,
Whenever you're right, shut up.
Ogden Nash

Keep your eyes open before marriage, half shut
afterwards. *Benjamin Franklin*

A happy marriage is a long conversation which
always seems too short. *Andre Maurois*

Marriage

Happy marriages begin when we marry the one we love, and they blossom when we love the one we marry. Communicating frequently and intimately is the best prescription for a successful marriage. Sustain your marriage with a sincere desire to meet your spouse's needs, not to have your needs met. Although we can never fully meet someone's needs, fulfilment is experienced when we see how close we can come. Being caring and sensitive to what is important to your spouse is a lifelong persevering commitment.

It has been said that in marriage being the right person is as important as finding the right person. Marriages are made in heaven, but *we* are responsible for the maintenance work!

Meanness

Remember the end never really justifies the
meanness. *Anon*

Misers are no fun to live with but they make great
ancestors. *Tom Snyder*

There are many things that we would throw away, if
we were not afraid that others might pick them up.
Oscar Wilde

Meanness

Meanness is one of those human characteristics
that is a double evil. Mean people not only cheat
those around them; they cheat themselves. To be
mean, to hold on to what you have in the face of
a world of need, is to dry up your heart and make a
desert out of your soul.

Meanness is particularly inappropriate in those
who believe in a God who gives. Such people have
experienced God's costly generosity by the ton, yet
they themselves can only bring themselves to offer
it to others by the gram.

Meanness is one of many conditions that brings
its own punishment. The real tragedy of being mean
is that ultimately you lose the only possessions that
are really valuable. To be mean is to be given the
great present of life and to get no further than filling
your hands with the wrapping paper.

Mistakes

To make no mistakes is not in the power of man,
but from their errors and mistakes the wise and
good learn wisdom for the future. *Plutarch*

Flops are a part of life's menu, and I've never been a
girl to miss out on any of the courses.
Rosalind Russell

The greatest mistake you can make in life is to be
continually fearing you will make one.
Elbert Hubbard

If we don't learn from our mistakes, there is no sense in making them. There is nothing wrong with making mistakes – just don't respond with encores!

There's a story about an executive at IBM who took the initiative on the development of a new product. The product was a risky venture that ended up a colossal failure and cost the company $10 million. IBM president Thomas Watson called the executive into his office, saying there was something he wanted to discuss with him.

The executive blurted out: 'I guess you want my resignation?'

Watson replied: 'You must be kidding. We have just spent $10 million educating you.'

Anyone making a multi-million-dollar mistake had to learn something that would help him do a better job next time.

I have heard that several management consultants would not promote anyone into a high-level job and responsibility who haven't made mistakes and learnt from their mistakes in their career development.

Have patience with others and yourself. Never confuse your mistakes with your value as a human being. You are a valuable, worthwhile person because you exist and no amount of trials or tribulations can change that.

Money

Money won't buy happiness, but it will pay the salaries of a huge research staff to study the problem. *Bill Vaughan*

I was happier when doing a mechanic's job. *Henry Ford*

Make all you can, save all you can, give all you can. *John Wesley*

Money is a powerful tool for doing good. Money's very ability to buy things, employ people and alleviate distress gives it almost 'god'-like powers. With those powers comes the inevitable risk that we will worship money by putting it on that throne in our lives that only God can safely sit on. And as a false 'god', money is one of the worst, encouraging us to measure everything in terms of profit and loss and blinding us to the things of true worth.

So how can money best be handled? One good rule is that we need to remind ourselves of money's limits. Money's power is selective: it may buy pleasure, but it doesn't buy happiness. It does little or nothing for any character we have, and may indeed make us worse. It is not even a guarantor of a longer and healthier life. Actually, the very best way of reducing the influence of money on our lives is a drastic one: it is to give away as much of it as we can afford; and then maybe some more on top. Nothing else is as successful in breaking money's power over us.

Morals

Morality and immorality are not defined by man's changing attitudes and social customs. They are determined by the God of the universe, whose timeless standards cannot be ignored with impunity.
James Dobson

People are very inclined to set moral standards for others. *Elizabeth Drew*

To educate a man in mind and not in morals is to educate a menace to society.
Theodore Roosevelt

Art, like morality, consists in drawing the line somewhere. *G. K. Chesterton*

This country has spent about 30 years trying very hard to prove that no one, not even children, should be fettered by anyone else's idea of proper

behaviour. Now we have no norms. Or at least none that we hold in common. Are we happy yet?
The Wall Street Journal, editorial, 1999

We are all, to some extent, moral people. Whenever we say something such as 'He shouldn't have done that' or 'What she did was so wrong' we are making a moral judgement. The idea of a society without any moral values is about as feasible (and as desirable) as having a road traffic system without any rules. There has to be some sort of shared values so that we can agree on what is right and wrong.

The question of the basis of our personal morality is inescapably linked to what we see the meaning of the universe to be. Moral values do not come from nowhere: they come from religious and philosophical systems. The rules of life come from God, and if you do not believe in God then you must find some other way of constructing a moral system. What cannot be done is to conjure up some system of beliefs out of thin air and declare them 'common values'. One of the most important questions about the future of countries such as Britain is how long the consensus of moral values can survive in the absence of the Christian faith that gave rise to it. Trees that have been uprooted rarely bear fruit.

N

Nature

Nature is the art of God. *Dante*

I have never been happier, more exhilarated, at peace, rested, inspired, and aware of the grandeur of the universe and the greatness of God than when I find myself in a natural setting not much changed from the way he made it. *Jimmy Carter*

Nature is wonderful and we all know that we ought to preserve nature, but does it teach us anything? Perhaps the most important thing that nature teaches is humility. We see all around us things that are too complex for us to understand, too wonderful for us to make and too immense for us to comprehend. In nature's vastness, human arrogance is silenced.

There is more in nature. The awesome and beautiful complexities of nature point at the existence of a Maker. Yet they do it gently: nature hints at God's presence. It doesn't demand that we believe in him.

Nature has tremendous value. To injure it is a double tragedy. We not only damage something of enormous value, we ruin something which has a message that we badly need to hear.

New Year

A New Year's resolution usually goes in one year
and out the next. *Anon*

God bless your year.
Your coming in, your travelling about.
The tough, the smooth,
The bright, the drear.
God bless your year.
Albert Wells

Be at war with your vices, at peace with your
neighbours, and let every new year find you a better
person. *Benjamin Franklin*

January is the month of beginnings. *Janua* in Latin
means a door. From it came the name of Janus,
ancient Roman symbol of all beginnings. Janus had
two faces so that he might look both forward and
back at the same time. He presided over gateways,
bridges, doors and entrances. In his honour, the first
month of the year was called January by Pompilius
in the seventh century before Christ.

You can never change the past. But you can
change the future. So remember those things which
will help you forward and let go of those things
which will only hold you back.

Obstacles

If you find a path with no obstacles, it probably doesn't lead anywhere. *Frank Clarke*

Obstacles cannot crush me; every obstacle yields to stern resolve. *Leonardo da Vinci*

When everything seems to be going against you, remember that the airplane takes off against the wind, not with it. *Henry Ford*

Obstacles

In 1982, mountain climbers Hugh Herr and Jeffrey Batzer were climbing Mount Washington. As they pushed for the summit, they stumbled into a blinding blizzard. They survived three days and nights in gale-force winds and below freezing temperatures. Although they came out of the ordeal alive, Jeffrey Batzer ended up losing one leg and Hugh Herr lost both.

Doctors warned Hugh Herr about the limitations he would have to accept. Instead, he designed artificial limbs that enabled him to continue climbing. He invented a more comfortable socket for leg prostheses. And he became an advocate for technological solutions to physical disabilities with the objective of designing legs to enable those who are disabled to run marathons.

Opportunity

We are faced with great opportunities brilliantly disguised as impossible situations.
Chuck Swindoll

When one door closes, another opens. But we often look so long and so regretfully upon the closed door that we do not see the one which has opened for us. *Helen Keller*

Opportunity is missed by most people because it is dressed in overalls and looks like work.
Thomas A. Edison

Opportunity

Many of us have heard opportunity knocking at our doors, but by the time we have turned the burglar alarm off, pushed back the bolts, turned the locks — it was gone. The older you get, the longer it takes to get to the door if opportunity knocks. Opportunity knocks, but it has never been known to turn the handle and walk in!

Opportunity is like a moving target, and the bigger the opportunity, the faster it moves. The opportunity is frequently lost because of deliberating. Opportunities seem to multiply as they are seized.

Opportunity is defined as a possibility that presents itself and can either be grasped or lost. The trouble with opportunity is that it's always more recognisable going than coming. Be grateful for the doors of opportunity and for the friends who oil the hinges.

Optimism and Pessimism

A pessimist sees the difficulty in every opportunity; an optimist sees the opportunity in every difficulty. *Winston Churchill*

A pessimist is someone who feels bad when he feels good for fear he'll feel worse when he feels better. *Thomas Jefferson*

Pessimists always take the cynical route. *Antoni Tabok*

There seems to be a great division in the human race between the pessimists and the optimists. One of the big questions in life is which of these is the right view? Most of us find it hard to disagree with the realism of the pessimist position yet, at the same time, we recognise that optimism is the better system to live by; a life is best filled with happiness not gloom. Billy Graham's comment on the question is worth pondering: 'If I didn't have spiritual faith, I would be a pessimist. But I'm an optimist. I've read the last page in the Bible. It's all going to turn out all right.'

P

Passion

The most powerful weapon on earth is the human soul on fire. *Ferdinand Foch*

When you set yourself on fire, people love to come and see you burn. *John Wesley*

Without passion man is a mere latent force and possibility, like the flint which awaits the shock of the iron before it can give forth its spark. *Amiel*

One person with passion is better than forty people merely interested. *Attributed to E. M. Forster*

Passion

We are ambivalent about passion. On the one hand we are inclined to be suspicious of passion. After all, to have passion is to be only one step away from being a fanatic and no one wants to be one of those. And our society celebrates 'coolness' and the very essence of coolness is not to be passionate about anything. There is also a certain intellectual logic to our caution about passion. If you believe that nothing is really true and nothing is really false, then any sort of passion seems ludicrous. Why get worked up about anything when the world is meaningless?

Yet, on the other hand, we also realise that without passion nothing is accomplished and no one is convinced. Deep down, we actually have a grudging respect for people who are passionate about things. Secretly, we envy their drive and vision. Is it possible that, deep down, we know that there really are serious issues in life, that the world does have a meaning and that there are things that we ought to be passionate about?

Patience

Patience is something you admire in the driver
behind you, but not in the one ahead.
Bill McGlashen

The strongest of all warriors are these – time and
patience. **Leo Tolstoy**

Our patience will achieve more than our force.
Edmund Burke

When God ripens apples, he isn't in a hurry and
doesn't make a noise. **D. Jackman**

Patience

Patience, along with such things as chastity and gentleness, is one of those traditional virtues that has now acquired almost Endangered Species status. 'Instant' is one of the keywords of our age: we want instant access, instant credit, instant communication and instant gratification. We want it all and we want it now. And, of course, to want something in an instant leaves no time for patience.

We need reminding that some things refuse to come in a hurry. Trees, gardens, the best wines, learning a language, gaining wisdom, a rewarding relationship; all these things take time and cannot be rushed. To reject patience is to miss out on some of the best things that life has to offer. We must learn that, like farmers, we can't sow and reap the same day. Rome was not built in a day!

Peace

All men desire peace, but very few desire those
things that make for peace.
Thomas à Kempis

Do your best and then sleep in peace. God is
awake. *Anon*

Serenity is not freedom from the storm, but peace
amid the storm. *Anon*

We experience two sorts of peace; what we can call 'peace of life' and 'peace of mind'. Peace of life is all to do with external circumstances; it occurs in the absence of wars, squabbles and disputes. Peace of mind or inner peace is something that is harder to define; it depends on the absence of mental or spiritual turmoil. Strangely, the two sorts of peace are largely independent of each other. You can have inner peace in the most turbulent of settings and you can be in the most tranquil and prosperous situations and have no inner peace whatsoever.

In a troubled world, we need to be peacemakers, and to make it a priority to do all that we can to bring harmony to people and nations, even if the only areas we can work in are those of our family and our workplace. What the world needs is peace that passes all misunderstanding. And gaining inner peace is essential. After all, if we do not have peace in our hearts then no achievement in life is worthwhile and if we do have peace, then no failure will trouble us.

The pursuit of inner peace defeats many people. Finding inner peace involves dealing with the great issues of life: its meaning and purpose. Above all, finding a lasting and durable inner peace is only found by knowing God.

And there will be no peace as long as God remains unseated at the conference table.

Perseverance

The rewards for those who persevere far exceed
the pain that must precede the victory.
Ted Engstrom

Great works are performed not by strength, but by
perseverance. *Samuel Johnson*

There are very few problems that pure, dogged
perseverance won't eventually solve.
Zig Ziglar

Perseverance is not a long race; it is many short
races, one after another. *Walter Elliot*

It's often the last key on the ring that opens the door. The word 'persevere' comes from the prefix 'per', meaning through, coupled with the word 'severe'. It means to keep pressing on, even through severe circumstances.

In 1914, Thomas Edison's factory was destroyed by fire. Much of Edison's life's work went up in smoke. The next morning Edison looked at the ruins and said: 'There is great value in disaster. All our mistakes are burned up. Thank God we can start anew.'

Three weeks after the fire, Thomas Edison delivered the first phonograph.

Edmund Burke said: 'Never despair, but if you do, WORK ON IN DESPAIR.'

Potential

Many people are restrained in thoughts, actions and results. They never move further than the boundaries of their self-imposed limitation.
John C. Maxwell

If you deliberately plan to be less than you are capable of being, then I warn you that you'll be unhappy. You'll be evading your own capacities, your own possibilities. *Abraham Maslow*

To be what we are, and to become what we are capable of becoming, is the only end of life.
Robert Louis Stevenson

The Japanese carp called Koi is a fascinating fish. If you keep it in a small fish bowl, it will grow up to 3 inches long. Take the Koi out and place it in a larger tank and the Koi will grow up to 6 inches. Put the same Koi into a pond and it will grow up to 18 inches, and then place the Koi into a lake where it can really stretch out and it has the potential of reaching up to 36 inches long.

The Koi always has the potential to be 36 inches long but is restricted by the environment it which it finds itself. Sometimes we are restricted by the environment we are in, and other times we choose to play safe in the pond when we should be in the lake. Unless we expand who we are, we will always have what we have got.

Power

Nearly all men can stand adversity, but if you want
to test a man's character, give him power.
Abraham Lincoln

The power of man has grown in every sphere,
except over himself. *Winston Churchill*

The nineteenth-century historian Lord Acton said, 'Power corrupts and absolute power corrupts absolutely.' It is a statement that is all too easy to believe but one that, in reality, is an over-simplification. Power itself is neutral. It can be used for good, to build up, heal and liberate, or for evil, to destroy, hurt and enslave. What power does is amplify what we are as human beings. So some people, given power, simply help more people than they are already doing. And sadly, other people, given power, will hurt people instead. But power itself does not corrupt.

So why does power so often produce more negative than positive results? The answer is that corruption does not arise from power; it already exists in the human heart. Power just magnifies it. That is why those societies that have respected the Bible's analysis of human nature as being twisted and turned in on itself, have built in checks and balances to prevent the abuse of power. Ironically, the issue of power focuses not on what we control, but on what controls us.

Prayer

Prayer is the contemplation of the facts of life from the highest point of view.
Ralph Waldo Emerson

I have been driven many times to my knees by the overwhelming conviction that I had nowhere else to go. My own wisdom, and that of all about me, seemed insufficient for the day.
Abraham Lincoln

Prayer is not merely an occasional impulse to which we respond when we are in trouble; prayer is a life attitude. *Walter Mueller*

Pray as you can, not as you can't. *Dom Chapman*

What we need is a desire to know the whole will of God, with a fixed resolution to do it.
John Wesley

Prayer is communicating with God. Through prayer we come to know the all-powerful and loving God and who he is; through prayer we allow God to direct our lives. Prayer shapes our lives.

Given that prayer is so important and that it is so central to what we are as human beings, it was natural for Jesus' followers to ask him to teach them how to pray. He answered them by giving the prayer that the Church for centuries has called 'The Lord's Prayer':

Our Father in heaven,
hallowed be your name,
your kingdom come,
your will be done,
on earth as it is in heaven.
Give us today our daily bread.
Forgive us our debts,
as we also have forgiven our debtors.
And lead us not into temptation,
but deliver us from the evil one.
The Bible – Matthew 6:9–13

Pride

Pride makes us artificial and humility makes us real.
Thomas Merton

Pride is the only disease known to man that makes everyone sick except the one who has it.
Bud Robinson

None are so empty as those who are full of themselves. *Benjamin Whichcote*

God sends no one away empty, except those who are full of themselves. *D. L. Moody*

Many people find it surprising that, in Christianity, pride is held up as one of the most dangerous of vices. Surely, some people protest, isn't pride no more than an annoying and foolish personality trait? No, pride is a mask – it is excessive self-esteem and conceit, an exaggerated opinion of oneself.

Pride is serious because proud people fail to see that there is anything wrong with them and, of course, those who are not prepared to admit that they're ill never look for a cure. The Bible states that: 'Pride goes before destruction, a haughty spirit before a fall' (Proverbs 16:18). 'Many a bee has been drowned in its own honey.' It is good for us to swallow our pride and console ourselves with the knowledge that it is 100 per cent calorie free! Be humble or you will stumble.

Problems

Progress implies both new and continuing problems and, unlike Presidential administrations, problems rarely have terminal dates.
Dwight D. Eisenhower

If the only tool you have is a hammer, you tend to see every problem as a nail.
Abraham Maslow

One half of our problems can be traced to saying 'Yes' too quickly and not saying 'No' soon enough.
Josh Billings

Don't find fault. Find a remedy. *Henry Ford*

The problem is never how to get new, innovative thoughts into your mind, but how to get old ones out. *Dee Hock*

For every problem
Under the sun
There is a solution
Or there is none.
If there's a solution
Go and find it.
If there isn't,
Never mind it.

Anon

Problems

Frequently, it is not problems themselves that are the difficulty; it is the way we approach them that does the real harm. There are many helpful hints for tackling problems; these are just a few:

- Don't waste time in recrimination. Many people expend a lot of energy in apportioning blame because it is easier to do than solving the problem.
- Don't fix the blame, fix the problem.
- Avoid panic. Panic never solves anything and frequently makes things worse.
- Get the right perspective on the matter. Appearances can be deceptive; some spectacular problems can be trivial and some things that seem to be of little importance can, ultimately, be disastrous.
- Analyse the problem. What is going on? Why? Which issues need dealing with now? Which can wait?
- Take advice. Never be too proud to ask for help.

- Act decisively. Delay can make matters worse. As the saying goes: 'You don't drown by falling in the water; you drown by staying there.'
- Learn from what happened. When the problem is solved, take some time to make sure it doesn't happen again.
- Above all, be positive. View problems as challenges to be surmounted. And don't run away from problems – running from problems is a sure way of running into problems.

Quality

Quality is not an act. It is a habit. *Aristotle*

It is better to deserve honours and not have them, than to have them and not deserve them.
Mark Twain

Good is not good where better is expected.
Thomas Fuller

Quality

Many of us can't tell the difference between eighteen-carat gold and fourteen-carat gold. Some of us can't even tell the difference between solid gold and gold plate. In old London town, the jewellers of Goldsmith's Hall took great pride in the quality of their work. They wanted each customer to know exactly what they were buying. So they devised a mark of quality, the 'hallmark', and its use became established by law. When a piece of gold was stamped with a crown and the figure 18, it was eighteen-carat gold. The 'mark of the hall' guaranteed it.

We need to mark a stamp of quality, a hallmark, a guarantee that our products are genuine.

Quietness

I have never been hurt by anything I didn't say.
Calvin Coolidge

I regret often that I have spoken; never that I have
been silent. *Syrus*

An inability to stay quiet is one of the most
conspicuous failures of mankind.
Walter Bagehot

It's probably true that if people do not understand our silence, they probably don't understand our words. It's ironic that we say, 'Silence is golden,' but we can't be quiet!

The desert fathers of centuries ago understood the importance of a silent environment. They would say, 'Fuge, terche et quisset' – silence, solitude and inner peace.

We must learn to soundproof our minds and hearts against the intruding noises of the world in order to hear what God has to say.

Anne Frank wrote in her diary on 23rd February 1944:

> The best remedy for those who are afraid,
> lonely or unhappy is to go outside,
> somewhere where they can be quiet, alone
> with the heavens, nature and God. Because
> only then does one feel that all is as it should
> be.

R

Resilience

Resilience is the capacity for recovery.
Sherry Lowry

A cheerful look brings joy to the heart.
The Bible — Proverbs 15:30

I get up when I fall down. **Paul Harvey**

Resilience is the capacity for recovery. It is our capacity to retain a positive attitude. Resilience is the ability to get through, get over and thrive after trauma, trials and tribulations. Resiliency is the ability to bounce back.

Instead of asking why bad things happen to good people, let's focus on how good people can best overcome bad events and situations.

The book *Pollyanna* by Eleanor Porter is about a girl whose father, a minister, died, leaving her orphaned. Her only relative was an unpleasant and severe aunt who took her in. Pollyanna was an optimist who somehow managed to find a bright side to everything. Her favourite word was 'glad', and she enjoyed her 'glad game' in which she tried to find something in every situation, no matter how bad, to be glad about.

Pollyanna's cheerfulness eventually began to transform her aunt into a pleasant and loving person and, in fact, the whole town became a different place because of Pollyanna.

The word 'Pollyanna' is listed in Webster's dictionary as 'someone who is excessively happy'.

Responsibility

I believe that we are solely responsible for our choices, and we have to accept the consequences of every deed, word, and thought throughout our lifetime. *Elisabeth Kubler-Ross*

One of the annoying things about believing in free will and individual responsibility is the difficulty in finding someone to blame your troubles on. And when you do find someone, it's remarkable how often their picture turns up on your driver's license. *P. J. O'Rourke*

The price of greatness is responsibility. *Winston Churchill*

Responsibilities gravitate to the person who can shoulder them. *Elbert Hubbard*

Responsiblity

We live in an age when we prefer to dodge personal responsibility. It is all too common to hear people blame their genes, their diet, their parents or their upbringing for what they are or what they have done. Almost anything is preferable to saying, 'It's my fault.' Such excuses are understandable; they shift the blame nicely.

It is easy to dodge our responsibilities, but we cannot dodge the consequences of dodging our responsibilities. And by doing this we are saying that we are not in control of our lives. In effect, we are admitting that we are no more than victims, pawns pushed around on a chessboard or cogs in a machine. It is a high price for an excuse: if we surrender our responsibility, we surrender our humanity. It is our responsibilities, not ourselves, that we should take seriously.

s

Self-control

The first and best victory is to conquer self.
Plato

Freedom is obtained not by the enjoyment of what is desired but by controlling desire itself.
Epictetus

What lies in our power to do, also lies in our power not to do. *Aristotle*

Not being able to govern events, I govern myself.
Michel de Montaigne

Self-control is love holding the reins.
Donald Grey Barnhouse

Raynald III was a fourteenth-century duke. He was grossly overweight and his brother imprisoned him in a room that was built around him. The room had no bars on the windows and no lock on the doors. The only problem was that the door was smaller than normal size, and so, due to his size, Raynald III could not squeeze through the opening and set himself free.

Yet there was still hope: if Raynald could lose enough weight, he could go free. But Raynald loved to eat more than anything in the world. Each day, a variety of delicious food was sent to Raynald's room. Instead of growing thinner, he grew fatter. He was a prisoner not of locks and bars, but of his own appetite.

Self-control is the restraint exercised over our impulses, emotions and desires. It is the capacity for keeping our words and actions under control. Without self-control we create trouble for ourselves.

Sincerity

What is uttered from the heart alone will win the hearts of others to your own. *Goethe*

Sincerity – an openness of heart.
François de La Rochefoucauld

Sincerity makes the least man to be of more value than the most talented hypocrite.
Charles Spurgeon

The word 'sincerity' in Greek means 'judged in the sunlight' and the English word is derived from the Latin *sine cera*, which means 'without wax'. In the days when art flourished in ancient Greece, it was common practice to repair with 'invisible' wax any vase or statue that had been damaged. A person of high rank might employ a sculptor to chisel their bust in marble. Sometimes, if the chisel slipped, the end of the nose would be chipped off. Rather than go to all the trouble of making a new bust, a sculptor would mend the features with wax. They would then sell the defective workmanship. If the client was wise, he would carry the finished statuette into the sunlight and examine it carefully. If he didn't, the nose might drop off his statuette in the heated room of his house. If this happened, the statue was not 'sincere', i.e. not 'without wax', and could not bear careful scrutiny in the sunlight.

Stress

Sometimes I get the feeling the whole world is
against me, but deep down I know that's not true.
Some of the smaller countries are neutral.
Robert Orben

Most stress is caused by people who overestimate
the importance of their problems.
Michael LeBoeuf

When you get to the end of your rope, tie a knot,
hang on and swing. *Leo Buscaglia*

Many experiences in life cause stress. These 'stressors' create 'eustress', i.e. healthy, positive stress, or 'distress', i.e. unhealthy, negative stress. Our bodies are designed to meet these stressors of either kind. However, we must determine what is the right amount of stress for us to function at our optimum level. Experiencing too little stress causes irritability, boredom, lethargy and apathy. However, too much stress can produce the same results and that feeling that you are on the verge of caving in.

Beware of putting too many irons in the fire, otherwise the fire will go out. Someone said that, 'If your output exceeds your input, then your upkeep will be your downfall.' Sometimes we just have to say 'Enough is enough!' and create some balance in our lives.

Success

No one ever attains success by simply doing what is required of them. *Charles Kendall Adams*

The secret to success is to do the common things uncommonly well. *John D. Rockefeller*

Sometimes it is not good enough to do your best; you have to do what's required.
Winston Churchill

If A equals success, then the formula is A = X + Y + Z, where X is work, Y is play and Z is keeping your mouth shut. *Albert Einstein*

There are no secrets to success. It is the result of preparation, hard work, and learning from failure.
Colin Powell

Many people get criticised because, it is claimed, they are 'hungry for success'. In fact, the criticism is unfair. What is probably really being criticised is the manner in which they are seeking success. All too often, what lies behind such complaints is envy.

In fact, the biggest danger is not that too many people seek success; it is that too few do. So many people are content with mediocrity, with being in 'survival mode' and with doing no more than enough to avoid failure. This is not just a problem of work ethics, it is a problem elsewhere. For instance, many people have no higher ambition for their marriages than for them to survive; to aim at success is beyond them.

Yet success, of the right sort and gained in the right way, is something that we must strive for. If we don't strive for success, we must expect failure!

Suffering

It is by those who have suffered that the world has been advanced. *Leo Tolstoy*

The truth that many people never understand, is that the more you try to avoid suffering the more you suffer because smaller and more insignificant things begin to torture you in proportion to your fear of being hurt. *Thomas Merton*

He who fears he shall suffer, already suffers what he fears. *Michel de Montaigne*

Although the world is full of suffering, it is full also of the overcoming of it. *Helen Keller*

Suffering

Some cultures embrace and honour suffering; ours shuns it. In contemporary thinking, pleasure is the ultimate good and therefore suffering is disastrous.

This is not only a fallacy but a dangerous fallacy. History shows us that nothing great was ever achieved without someone being prepared to suffer. In fact, in most cases nothing great was achieved without someone undergoing suffering. Of course, suffering is unpleasant and to be avoided where possible but avoiding it is often not possible. If we want to do what is right or even to simply succeed, we must accept that we may have to suffer. It is not simply that there is no gain without pain, but by refusing to accept any pain, we effectively give up before we have even started. Some plants produce a beautiful fragrance, but they only produce a beautiful fragrance when they are crushed. May that be true of us when we are crushed.

T

Temptation

There are several good protections against
temptations, but the surest is cowardice. It is easier
to stay out than get out. *Mark Twain*

Call on God, but row away from the rocks.
Ralph Waldo Emerson

No man knows how bad he is until he has tried to
be good. There is a silly idea about, that good
people don't know what temptation means.
C. S. Lewis

The whole subject of temptation has been trivialised beyond belief so that today when most people think of temptation they think of a slimmer who is faced with a pile of chocolates.

Yet temptation is a real and serious issue. It occurs whenever we are faced with two possibilities: to do what is difficult and right, or to do what is easy and wrong. Some temptations are blatant and obvious and others, perhaps the most dangerous, are subtle and well disguised. We all face many real temptations each day; some temptations are trivial, for instance whether to lie in bed instead of going for a jog, while others are extraordinarily serious: to cheat, steal or hurt someone.

How we deal with temptation is not just a matter of whether we do what is right. Every temptation is like a fork in the road of life. Every time we defeat temptation we move along the right road of life; every time we give in to temptation we divert ourselves further away from what we ought to be. It is better to shun the bait than to struggle on the hook. How we respond to temptation affects the sort of people we become.

Thanksgiving

The person who has stopped being thankful has fallen asleep in life. *Robert Louis Stevenson*

It is always possible to be thankful for what is given rather than to complain about what is not given. One or the other becomes a habit of life. *Elisabeth Elliot*

No action can be truly complete without gratitude. A symphony without applause at the end isn't a completed symphony. *Peter Stewart*

Thanksgiving

Thanksgiving Day, observed on the fourth Thursday of November, has been a national holiday in the USA since 1863. On this day, Americans remember with gratitude the many blessings they have received.

In 1620, the first Pilgrims landed in Massachusetts. Their first year was difficult – food was scarce and supplies were low. Nearly half of the group died during the first winter. However, a Native-American called Squanto came to their aid. Squanto taught the people to plant and harvest crops in the new American climate and he led the people to a prosperous autumn. With great thankfulness the Pilgrims called for a thanksgiving feast to celebrate their bounty.

We never know all we should be grateful to God for.

Time

When a man sits with a pretty girl for an hour, it seems like a minute. But let him sit on a hot stove for a minute and it's longer than an hour. That's relativity. *Albert Einstein*

Time is the wisest of all counsellors. *Plutarch*

Half our life is spent trying to do something with the time we have rushed through life trying to save. *Will Rogers*

Nine-tenths of wisdom consists of being wise in time. *Theodore Roosevelt*

Time heals griefs and quarrels, for we change and are no longer the same person. *Pascal*

Teach us to number our days aright, that we may gain a heart of wisdom. *The Bible — Psalm 90:12*

Time

We may be able to measure time to billionths of a second well but we don't understand what it is. Is time a phenomenon, a property or a characteristic of life? No one knows. But what we do know is that time is our most important resource. It is also a diminishing one: decreasing at the rate of 24 hours every day. If you believe, in any way, that there is a meaning and purpose to your life, then time has an extraordinary value. The priceless nature of time is heightened by the fact that time cannot be bought.

Yet despite time's value, we still waste it, not in needful things like relaxation and sleep but in trivia, in meaningless or futile actions. In theory we are aware that the earth revolves, but in practice we do not perceive this because the ground on which we stand seems not to move. So it is with time in our lives. If time could be seen and held as if it were money, we would be far more concerned about how we handle it. We would be much less willing to see it slip through our fingers. Seize the day.

Truth

Peace if possible, truth at all costs. *Martin Luther*

If you tell the truth, you don't have to remember anything. *Mark Twain*

Fallacies do not cease to be fallacies because they become fashions. *G. K. Chesterton*

At least in theory, we all honour truth. But in practice we live in a world of 'truth-decay'. We often find that the truth is inconvenient and sometimes painful. Because the truth can hurt both those who hear the truth and those who tell it, we tend to settle for something more comfortable.

This desire to be comfortable is one of the greatest enemies of truth. When, in Hans Christian Andersen's story, the emperor paraded without any clothes on, the spectators were not taken in; they knew the so-called 'new suit' was a lie. But they stayed silent because it was more comfortable to agree with the king. The same peril continually occurs in real life; it is easier to go with the crowd than to disagree.

To stand up for truth is not easy; it can mean being made uncomfortable and it may be against our self-interest. Yet we need to remember that going against the truth, for any reason, is effectively participating in a lie.

Understanding

The wise are known for their understanding, and pleasant words are persuasive.
The Bible, New Living Translation – Proverbs 16:21

Everything that irritates us about others can lead us to an understanding of ourselves. **Carl Jung**

To understand others, you should get behind their eyes and walk down their spines. **Rod McKuen**

Understanding

There is an ancient story of a king who wanted to teach his four sons never to make rash judgements. The king instructed his eldest son to go during the winter season to see a mango tree, the second son to go during spring, the third in summer and the youngest in autumn.

After the last son returned from his autumn trip, the king called them all together to describe what they had seen. 'It looks like a dead old stump,' said the eldest. 'No,' said the second, 'it is green.' The third said it was 'as beautiful as a rose'. The youngest said, 'No, its fruit is like a pear.' 'Each was right,' said the king, 'for each of you saw the tree in a different season.'

The lesson is obvious: take time to understand, make sure you have all the facts, learn the background, and make sure you place yourself where others are.

Unselfishness

Man's highest life does not consist in self-expression, but in self-sacrifice. *R. H. Benson*

The love of liberty is the love of others; the love of power is the love of ourselves. *William Hazlitt*

We are more troublesome to ourselves than anyone else is to us. *St Francis de Sales*

Don't be selfish; don't try to impress others. Be humble, thinking of others as better than yourselves. Don't look out only for your own interests, but take an interest in others, too.
The Bible, New Living Translation – Philippians 2:3–4

V

Values

A corporation's values are its lifeblood. Without effective communication, actively practised without the art of scrutiny, those values will disappear in a sea of trivial memos and impertinent reports.
Max De Pree

Always do right. This will gratify some people and astonish the rest. **Mark Twain**

Know what your values are and live in a way consistent with your values. **Danny Cox**

Values

Sister Carol Anne O'Marie was a nun who wrote mystery novels about an old nun playing detective. Sister Carol was approached by a film company to turn her stories into a television series.

Sister Carol was told by the company that it would help dramatically if the main character was younger, had a drinking problem and had a love affair with a married man before she became a nun. When Sister Carol declined to consider such changes the television producer resorted to the final temptation: 'You are turning down an opportunity of a lifetime, Sister, to make a lot of money.'

'What would I do with it?' replied the nun, who had taken a vow of poverty. 'I'm not going to live in a nicer convent.'

Vision

Vision is the art of seeing things invisible.
Jonathan Swift

A rock pile ceases to be a rock pile the moment a single man contemplates it, bearing within him the image of a cathedral. *Antoine de Saint-Exupéry*

The bravest are surely those who have the clearest vision of what is before them, glory and danger alike, and yet not withstanding, go out to meet it.
Thucydides

The Bible says, 'Where there is no vision, the people perish' (21st Century King James Version – Proverbs 29:18). In Numbers chapter 13 it is recorded how God sent Moses to lead the Israelites from captivity in Egypt, into the Promised Land. As the people approached the Promised Land, spies were sent ahead to evaluate the situation. One man from each of the twelve tribes was chosen for the scouting trip.

On their return, the scouting report created confusion. Ten of the spies saw giants who would crush them like grasshoppers. Two of them, Joshua and Caleb, on the other hand, saw 'a land flowing with milk and honey'.

'Let's go,' they said. The majority won because of their fear and as a result the people died in the wilderness – except two, Joshua and Caleb, who did enter the Promised Land.

God had already promised the Israelites safe entry. Yet even with a guaranteed vision clearly given to them, the Israelites, influenced by ten people, chose to play safe and live by their self-imposed limitations.

Today, many people overlook their opportunities

either because of a lack of faith or a lack of
determination and enthusiasm to pursue a vision –
and they are slowly decaying.

Wisdom

Wisdom is ofttimes nearer when we stoop, than when we soar. *William Wordsworth*

From the errors of others a wise man corrects his own. *Publius Syrus*

A wise old owl sat on an oak.
The more he saw, the less he spoke;
The less he spoke, the more he heard;
Why aren't we like that wise old bird?
Edward Hersey Richards

Wisdom

The wisdom of life is to change what we can, and to
  endure what we can't.

Wisdom is knowing what to do, with what we know.

Be wise with your thoughts; they can create words.

Be wise with your words; they can become actions.

Be wise with your actions; they can develop habits.

Be wise with your habits; they can affect character.

Be wise with your character; it can shape your
  destiny.

Wisdom is common sense to an uncommon degree.

Anon

Work

A dictionary is the only place where you will find success before work. *Anon*

Men for the sake of getting a living, forget to live. *Margaret Fuller*

No man on his deathbed ever looked up into the eyes of his family and friends and said: 'I wish I'd spent more time at the office.' *John Piper*

Work

Work is a significant part of our life. One of the greatest blessings in life is to have a fulfilling job. Yet it is precisely because work is so important that it has dangers attached to it.

One danger is of making work the central point of life so that we live to work rather than work to live. One reason why God included in the Ten Commandments a ruling that all work was to cease one day a week was, no doubt, to make the point that while our work is an important part of our lives, it is not our life.

Another danger is that it is very easy for us to let work define who we are. We have all been at meetings where the first question after we have been introduced to someone is, 'And what do you do?' Yet we are individuals first, and our job comes a long way after that. To define who we are on the basis of our work is to ask for an identity crisis when we are made redundant or retire. In God's eyes, our value does not change when we close the office door behind us for the last time.

Our work is important; but it is neither the meaning of life nor the basis of who we are.

Worry

Worry does not empty tomorrow of its sorrow. It empties today of its strength.
Corrie Ten Boom

Every evening I turn my worries over to God. He's going to be up all night anyway. **Mary Crowley**

Worry is like a rocking chair; it gives you something to do, but it doesn't get you anywhere.
Evan Esar

The Greek word for 'worry' literally means 'to be drawn in different directions'.

Worry is a small trickle of fear that meanders through the mind until it cuts a channel into which all other thoughts are drained.

Worry can become 'toxic' and make us sick. It can restrict our enjoyment of life and it can reduce our productivity. Toxic worry is harmful to us and to our well-being. It is a fact that worriers die sooner than non-worriers. The irony is that worry doesn't help us achieve anything.

We need to realise that many things come to all of us that we cannot do anything about.

Let's choose to worry less, and laugh more!

X

Xmas

Those who do not have Christmas in their heart,
will never find it under a tree. *Roy L. Smith*

God bless us, every one.
Tiny Tim (in Charles Dickens, **A Christmas
Carol)**

Twas the night before Christmas, when all through
    the house,
Not a creature was stirring, not even a mouse;
The stockings were hung by the chimney with care,
In hopes that St Nicholas soon would be there…
Happy Christmas to all, and to all a goodnight.
Clement C. Moore

A 'politically correct alternative' to 'Merry Christmas and a Happy New Year':

> Best wishes for an environmentally conscious, socially responsible, low stress, non-addictive, gender neutral, winter solstice holiday, practised with the most joyous traditions of the religious persuasion of your choice, but with respect for the religious persuasion of others who choose to practise their own religion as well as those who choose not to practise a religion at all; plus a fiscally successful, personally fulfilling, and medically uncomplicated recognition of the generally accepted calendar year, but not without due respect for the calendars of choice of the other cultures whose contributions have helped make our society great, without regard to age, race, creed, colour, religion, national origin, disability, political affiliation or sexual orientation!
>
> Anon

In those days Caesar Augustus issued a decree that a census should be taken of the entire

Roman world. (This was the first census that took place while Quirinius was governor of Syria.) And everyone went to his own town to register.

So Joseph also went up from the town of Nazareth in Galilee to Judea, to Bethlehem the town of David, because he belonged to the house and line of David. He went there to register with Mary, who was pledged to be married to him and was expecting a child. While they were there, the time came for the baby to be born, and she gave birth to her firstborn, a son. She wrapped him in cloths and placed him in a manger, because there was no room for them in the inn.
The Bible – Luke 2:1–7

X is the first letter of the Greek word for Christ. For the early Christians, most of whom spoke and wrote Greek, the word 'Xmas' signified 'Christ's Mass'.

Originally the 'X' was to remember the 'cross' of Christ, and people using the abbreviation were reminded of Jesus' death and of celebrating the hope he offers humankind by coming to earth.

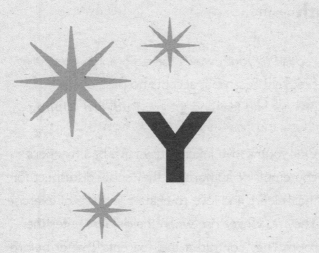

Youth

I speak to youth which can accomplish everything
precisely because it accepts no past, obeys no
present and fears no future. *Rudyard Kipling*

Our youths love luxury. They have bad manners,
contempt for authority – they show disrespect for
their elders and love to chatter in place of exercise.
They no longer rise when their elders enter the
room. They contradict their parents, chatter before
company, gobble up food, and tyrannise teachers.
Socrates, 400 BC

We cannot always build the future for our youth,
but we can build our youth for the future.
Franklin D. Roosevelt

Sometimes we give children information they are too young to understand. Like the seven-year-old who listened patiently to a talk about the birds and the bees, then turned to his Dad with a big smile. 'I get it,' he announced triumphantly, 'since I have a brother and a sister, you and Mum did it three times.'

We have speeded up the clock without being very helpful to adolescents. We teach them about fallopian tubes, but very little about the meaning of relationships and responsibility. Let us make it a priority to build children. It is far easier than mending broken adults. Let's give our youth roots and wings.

Z

Zeal

Zeal without knowledge is fire without light.
Thomas Fuller

Experience shows that success is due less to ability than to zeal. The winner is he who gives himself to his work, body and soul. *Charles Buxton*

Work with zeal, but give God the glory.
Henry Saulnier

Meryl Streep starred in a film called *Ironweed*. She played a ragged derelict that died in a cheap motel room. For more than 30 minutes before the scene, she hugged a bag of ice cubes in an agonised attempt to discover what it was like to be a corpse. When the cameras came on, she just lay there as Jack Nicholson cried and shook her limp body. One of the cameramen got concerned and said to the director, 'What's going on? She's not breathing!' When the director looked at her, he saw no signs of life, but he let the cameras roll. After the scene was filmed, she still didn't move. It took several minutes for her to come out of the state she had sunk herself into. The director said, 'Now that is acting with zeal.'

Meryl Streep's zeal for acting led her to go the extra mile and do the unthinkable in order to perform brilliantly.

Acknowledgements

Every effort has been made to trace and contact copyright holders and secure permission prior to printing. Hodder & Stoughton will be pleased to rectify any inadvertent errors or omissions in the next edition of this book.

The author and publisher would like to thank the following for permission to include quotes in this book:

Scott Adams, *The Dilbert Principle* (Boxtree, 1997). Used by permission.

Woody Allen, c/o Loeb & Loeb. Used by permission.

Winston Churchill, c/o Curtis Brown Ltd on behalf of the Estate of Winston S. Churchill. Used by permission.

Acknowledgements

Langston Hughes, c/o David Higham Associates, *Collected Poems of Langston Hughes* (Alfred A. Knopf, 1994). Used by permission.

E. Stanley Jones, c/o the United Christian Ashrams International on behalf of the author. Used by permission.

Eddy Ketchersid. Used by permission.

Vernon Law. Used by permission.

Michael LeBoeuf. Used by permission.

David McNally, *Even Eagles Need a Push* (Dell Publishing, 1994). Used by permission.

Thomas Merton, c/o the Merton Legacy Trust, *No Man Is an Island* (Shambhala, 2005) and *The Seven Storey Mountain* (SPCK Publishing, 1999). Used by permission.

George Orwell, *Nineteen Eighty Four*, c/o Bill Hamilton as the Literary Executor of the Estate of